DOCTOR ARCHIE

THE LIFE AND TIMES OF DOCTOR ARCHIBALD CAMERON

LAST MAN TO DIE FOR THE JACOBITE CAUSE

First published in 2014 by
For The Right Reasons
(Charity no. SC037781)
Printers & Publishers
60 Grant Street, Inverness
Email: fortherightreasons@rocketmail.com

British Library Cataloguing in Publication Data.
A catalogue record of this book is available from the British Library.

ISBN: 978-1-910205-01-3

Set in Verdana 11 and 10pt

DOCTOR ARCHIE

THE LIFE AND TIMES OF DOCTOR ARCHIBALD CAMERON

LAST MAN TO DIE FOR THE JACOBITE CAUSE

Mary McGrigor

Paul and Janet
With much love
Mary   March 2014

Foreword by
Donald Cameron of Lochiel
27th chief of Clan Cameron

About the Author

Mary McGrigor grew up in a fifteenth-century Scottish castle where she was captivated by a sense of the past. Authors like Scott and Buchan, and particularly R.L. Stevenson, increased her love of history and inspired an ambition to write. She married a soldier and 'followed the drum' until they bought a sheep farm in Argyll. Her first book, *The History of South Lochaweside,* written for an SWRI (Scottish Women's Institute) competition, was followed by *Dalmally and the Glens.* She then became a regular contributor to *Scottish Field* magazine, before writing *Argyll, Land of Blood and Beauty.* She has edited *The Family of Edmonstone of Duntreath* and *The Scalpel and the Sword,* the autobiography of her husband's famous ancestor, Sir James McGrigor, 'father' of the Royal Army Medical Corps. *Grass will not Grow on my Grave* investigates the notorious Appin Murder and the trial of James of the Glen. Further books are: *Rob Roy's Country, Paths of the Pilgrims, Defiant and Dismasted at Trafalgar, Wellington's Spies, Anna Countess of the Covenant* and *The Tsar's Doctor.*

--o0o--

For my sister

Fiona Cameron Rose

--o0o--

PREFACE AND ACKNOWLEDGEMENTS

I came across Doctor Archie while reading the family history of his friend and contemporary Sir Stuart Threipland, another of Prince Charles' doctors during his fateful campaign. Researching further I found that a full length biography does not exist to describe the life, work and above all the loyalty of a man who sacrificed both himself and his family to what he believed to be a rightful cause. I can only hope that my attempt to do so will do justice to the memory of this brave, self-effacing and most honest of men.

My first and warmest thanks must go to Donald Cameron of Lochiel for his kindness in writing the Foreword to this book. Among those who have helped with the writing and production I must thank Sonia Cameron Jacks, my fellow admirer of Doctor Archie, for the vast amount of work she has done in editing and preparing the manuscript for publication, and to Tearlach MacFarlane for his inestimable help. Also to Archie Mackenzie for his helpful suggestions; to Monsignor Thomas Wynne for allowing me to quote from his book 'The forgotten Cameron of the '45' and for the use of some of his photographs; to Iain Thornber for his unrivalled local knowledge; to Alex du Toit of the Fort William Museum; to Stephen Duffie for his lovely and evocative photographs, and finally to Jim Kirby of Polloch for information regarding Doctor Archie's connection with the Strontian Lead Mines. Lastly to the Reverend Richard Burkitt, publishing head of 'For the Right Reasons', a charity aimed at the rehabilitation of young people which continues in its success, and his Staff. To each and every one of these people my heartfelt gratitude extends.

Mary McGrigor
Upper Sonachan - Dalmally – Argyll December 2013

Contents

		page
	Foreword by Donald Cameron of Lochiel.	ix
1	The Camerons of Lochiel	1
2	The Inheritance	8
3	Sons without a Father	15
4	The Students	17
5	Loyalty and War	22
6	The Devil's Choice	27
7	The New Roads	31
8	The General Practitioner	33
9	Family Life	43
10	The Conference	46
11	The Summons	51
12	His Brother's Man	56
13	Preparations for War	61
14	The Ruthven Barracks	66
15	The Netherbow Port	70
16	Prestonpans	73
17	'Heaven's Darling'	77
18	'More Like Chimney Sweeps than Soldiers'	78
19	Falkirk	82
20	The Siege of Fort William	86
21	The Final Battle	90
22	Hunted Men	94
23	The Fatal Treasure	97
24	Gold for Guns	101
25	A Country on Fire	103
26	Capture and Escape	107
27	Ben Alder	110
28	The Prince Saved	113
29	The Haggis	119
30	Refugees in France	126
31	Versaille	131
32	Beyond the Pyrenees	136
33	Reunion	141
34	Rivals for Command	145

		page
35	The Jacobite Judas	150
36	Scotland	153
37	The Curse of the Gold	158
38	Betrayal	161
39	The Elibank Plot	167
40	Brenacoile	175
41	The Informer	180
42	The Tower of London	184
43	The Blunt Pencil	188
44	Last to Die for the Jacobite Cause	197
45	Aftermath	203

Appendix I		210
Appendix II	Dr Archibald Cameron's Memorial Concerning the Locharkaig Treasure (Stuart Papers. Vol.300 No 80)	211
Notes		214
Index		219
Bibliography		224
Pictures	between pages numbers 1-9 by courtesy of Monsignor Thomas Wynne Numbers 10-13 by Stephen Duffie	102-3
Map	The Highlands of Scotland	226-7

--o0o--

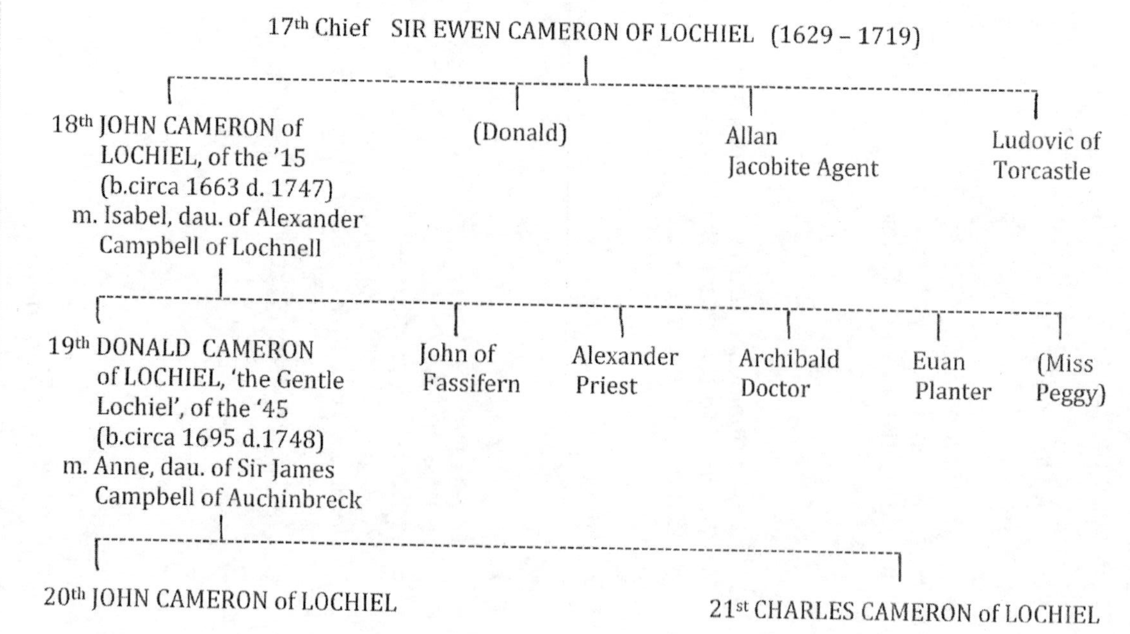

(with acknowledgements to John Stewart of Ardvorlich SCJ)

FOREWORD

Doctor Archie Cameron has always had a very special place in the history of Clan Cameron, not only because he was the last Jacobite to be executed but also because of his humanity, bravery and loyalty. Although reluctant to join the Rising of 1745, believing that it could not succeed, he joined his brother, the Gentle Lochiel, in that tragic enterprise. He tended the wounded of both sides, was a constant companion to his Chief and eventually helped him escape to France.

The intrigue and treachery surrounding the gold that was sent by the French in 1746 led to his betrayal and death in 1753. 'I am now ready to be offered; I have fought a good fight, all glory be to God'.

Because he was such a remarkable man, it is wonderful that this meticulously researched book has been written by my friend Mary McGrigor. It chronicles his life in the most compelling manner and tells the story of this universally loved and respected man with sympathy, academic excellence and understanding.

I am extremely grateful to Mary for all that she has done to shed light on Doctor Archie and I commend this book to clansfolk and all those interested in the Jacobites.

Donald Cameron of Lochiel
27th Chief of Clan Cameron

--o0o--

Doctor Archibald Cameron 1707-1753

Chapter 1
THE CAMERONS OF LOCHIEL

The year 1707 is remembered with mixed feelings in Scotland as that was when The Treaty of Union with England was formed. It was also the year in which Archibald, fourth son of John Cameron of Lochiel and his wife Isobel, a daughter of Alexander Campbell of Lochnell, was born.

The place of his birth was Achnacarry, the house built by his grandfather on a stretch of open meadow by the side of the river Arkaig where it plunges down from the loch of that name to Loch Lochy. Described as the finest house in the Highlands, it was built of logs hewn from Lochiel's own forests, only the chimney-stacks being constructed of stone.

Achnacarry, dominant in its position, epitomized the strength of its creator, chief of the Camerons of Lochiel. The great dark house, redolent of the wood of its creation, was dominated by his presence, the terrifying, legendary Sir Ewen Cameron, a man whom none in their senses would ever dare to defy. His grandchildren, the young Archie amongst them, grew up in reverence of his wrath.

They were not to realize, being only children, that the strength of the man they so greatly feared sprang from the dreadful events of his own childhood, which had made him the man he had become.

Known amongst his people as 'Sir Eoghain Dubh' Ewen had been born in 1629 in the Castle of Kilchurn, fortress of his mother's family, the Campbells of Glenorchy, standing below the massive mountain of Cruachan at the eastern end of Loch Awe. Brought up at first in the house of his foster-father, captain of the MacMartins, a sept of Clan Cameron, he was transferred, at the age of twelve, to the care of the 8th Earl, later the Marquis of Argyll, in the old castle of Inveraray on Loch Fyne.

Following the battle of Philiphaugh in September 1646, when Montrose was so disastrously defeated, Argyll forced the young Lochiel to witness the execution of three of the royalists whose dignity and courage on the scaffold reduced him to excessive grief. The horror of that day convinced him of the justice of the cause of Charles I.

In the spring of 1652, when only twenty years old but already outstandingly strong, Ewen was the first to rise for the Earl of Glencairn against Cromwell's army commanded by General Middleton. Later, when Monk had succeeded Middleton and came to Maryburgh (Fort William) he arranged for his soldiers to go on a timber felling expedition (presumably for building work at the Fort). Lochiel, receiving word that his best oak trees were being felled, took a band of trusty men to stop them. At Achdalieu on Locheilside there was a skirmish, during which he attacked the English officer. Together they wrestled on the ground, rolling down into the bed of a burn, which fortunately happened to be dry, where Lochiel, imprisoned under the weight of his opponent, managed to bite his throat out with his teeth, *'the sweetest bit I ever had in my life'* as afterwards he claimed.

Hearing that his own country was about to be invaded by the English from Inverness, Sir Ewen hastened back to Lochaber where he found MacDonell of Glengarry and MacDonald of Keppoch ready to raise their men in common defence of their lands. They agreed that having called their men to arms they would meet on a moor above Aberchalder, near Fort Augustus. Keppoch adhered to the arrangement but Glengarry defaulted *'walking and discoursing with the English Commander in the very centre of his troops'.*

Although Sir Ewen and MacDonell of Glengarry later fought together at Killiecrankie under Viscount Dundee, the treachery was never forgiven and remained the basis of an ongoing feud, disastrous to relationships between their descendants for over a hundred years.

In 1662 a dispute between the Camerons of Lochiel and the Mackintoshes, which had lasted for three and a half centuries, was finally ended when Mackintosh agreed to sell Glenlui and Loch Arkaig to Lochiel for the price of 12,500 merks. The Marquis of Athole had offered Lochiel the money to pay Mackintosh, but the 9th Earl of Argyll came up with easier terms, with the aim of obtaining the superiority of his lands.

Loyal to the Stuart king James II, or VII as he was known in Scotland, Lochiel actually joined the Marquis of Athole in taking control of Argyll's estates when, following his rebellion with Monmouth against the Catholic monarch, they were forfeited to the crown.

Again he fought for King James when, as William III sent an army to Scotland, he joined the force of the exiled king's champion, Viscount Dundee. Most famously, in 1689, by now aged sixty, at the battle of Killiecrankie he hurled off his shoes to lead his men to the victory which nevertheless ended with the death of Dundee.

Sir Ewen was by then the stuff of legend, a hero throughout the Highlands and not only to the members of his clan. Intolerant of any form of weakness, on one occasion when about to sleep in the snow, seeing one of his sons or nephews using a snowball as a pillow, he famously kicked it from under his head.

Lord Macaulay, who likened him to Louis the Fourteenth, eulogized him when he wrote:

> Sir Ewen Cameron of Lochiel, surnamed the Black, was, in personal qualities unrivalled among the Celtic Princes. He was a gracious master, a trusty ally, a terrible enemy...Lochiel was tall and strongly built. In agility and skill at his weapons he had few equals among the inhabitants of the hills.

> He had been repeatedly victorious in single combat, his clansmen looked on him with pride when they related how he had broken hostile ranks and hewn down tall warriors. He was a hunter of great fame. He made vigorous war on the wolves, which down to his time, preyed on the red deer of the Grampians; and by his hand perished the last of the ferocious breed, which is known to have wandered at large in our island. Nor was Lochiel less distinguished by intellectual than by bodily vigour. He might, indeed, have seemed ignorant to educated and travelled Englishmen, who had studied the Classics under Busby at Westminster, and under Aldrich at Oxford; who had learned something about the sciences among Fellows of the Royal Society, and something of the fine arts in the galleries of Florence and Rome. But although Lochiel had very little knowledge of books, he was eminently wise in council, eloquent in debate, ready in devising expedients, and skilful in managing the minds of men.[1]

In addition to all these qualities Sir Ewen had the gift of second sight. Early one morning the great house by the River Arkaig was thrown into commotion as the chief awoke, shouting to his wife that his king was landed and that his own son Allan was with him. No one dared to contradict him. On his orders a large bonfire was made, and the best liquor brought out to his lads (as he called his clansmen) that they might make merry and drink the king's health.[2]

They came, the men, their wives, their children and even their dogs, from far and wide to join in the great festivity. Sir Ewen's grandsons were there, Donald, a tall lad of sixteen, but still not his grandfather's height, John, some two years younger, Alexander, always full of joie de vivre, the life and soul of the party, Archie, then just nine, quieter and more serious than his brother, and finally Euan, not yet eight years old.

It was a joyous and bibulous occasion, which continued '*with uncommon festivity and mirth until the next day was nearly spent*'. The party goers were in some cases still recovering when news reached Achnacarry that King James, or the Chevalier as he was termed, had indeed landed at Peterhead, on 22nd December 1715, attended by Allan Cameron, at exactly the time that his father had seen him in his dream.

In those times, when open-handed hospitality was the main obligation of a chief, a guest of Lord Lovat at Castle Dounie described his surprise at what he found:

> His hall was crowded by visitors, vassals and tenants of all ranks, and the table which extended right down it, was covered at different places, with different kinds of meat and drink; though of each kind there was always a great abundance. At the head of the table the lords and lairds pledged him with claret (*which he got from France in exchange for salmon);* the tacksmen *(tenants)* drank port or whisky punch; the husbandmen refreshed themselves with strong beer and, at the door, a multitude of clansmen without shoes or bonnets, regaled themselves with bread, onions or a little cheese and small beer.[3]

Sir Ewen presided over these gatherings at Achnacarry where the deer and oxen and all kinds of wild fowl were roasted to feed his guests. The claret and brandy, both imported from the Continent at the cost of 15s per dozen bottles and brought over in panniers on horseback from the port of Leith, were consumed in great quantity. Toast after toast was drunk, first to the Stuart kings, until most of the men went to sleep, in beds or on the floor, wherever they could lay their heads.

One neighbour, notable for his absence at the gatherings at Achnacarry, was Cameron of Glennevis, a man persistent in maintaining a long-standing family feud. At the root of the problem was his unbreakable belief that his family were really Macdonalds who had held their land under Somerled long before any Camerons had appeared on the scene and, because of this, he refused to acknowledge the suzerainty of Lochiel, his family until recently having held their lands under the Gordon Earls of Huntly, overlords of Lochaber for several hundred years. Dislike between these two branches of the Cameron clan had simmered on for many years, the sons of Glennevis embittered by what they took to be the unfair discrimination of the senior house of Cameron, embodied in the person of Sir Ewen Dubh.

Sir Ewen, at the time of the exiled king's landing, was in his eighty-eighth year. Two years later, when MacGregor Drummond of Balhaldie came to visit him *'so great was his strength at that time that he wrung some blood from the point of my fingers with a grasp of his hand.'* Balhaldie described the amazing vitality of a man at what in those days was a very advanced age:

> Sir Ewen's eyes retained their former vivacity, and his sight was so good in his ninetieth year that he could discern the most minute object and read the smallest print; nor did he so much as want a tooth, which seemed as white and close as one would have imagined they were in the twentieth year of his age...He enjoyed continued perfect health from the cradle to the grave, except the flux by which means he was laid up during the whole of the year 1674; and not a drop of his blood was ever drawn, except on one occasion when a knife had accidentally pierced his foot.[4]

But human life is as unpredictable as it is fallible. Some three months after this the patriarch of Clan Cameron suffered a severe stroke. Lying in a cradle, rocked as a child, he is said to have been suckled on woman's milk before he died. Sir Walter Scott, who questioned this in his *Tales of a Grandfather,* could find no verification but did discover that he turned himself about in bed by means of a rope and pulley having lost the use of his lower limbs. In February 1719, he died of a high fever, *'though it had left him a few hours before his death when his memory and judgement returned'.*[5] His eldest son John succeeded him as the eighteenth Cameron of Lochiel.

Chapter 2
THE INHERITANCE

The great wooden house of Sir Ewen's creation lay shrouded and silent following his death. His grandchildren talked in whispers, overawed by the loss of the man whose overpowering presence had suddenly vanished from their lives. Soon, as his aura seemed to vanish slowly, as though reluctant to leave the place where its dominance had for so long ruled, they began to talk in normal voices again, growing more strident as they started squabbling, competitive as siblings in a large family usually are, and now relieved of the presence of the all powerful grandfather at the sound of whose roar of command they had formerly, immediately, been quiet.

Unsurprisingly, as so often happens to the follower of an immensely popular and powerful man, John Cameron of Lochiel was overshadowed by his father's fame. Born c1664, he must have been a large child for his foot would not fit the fairy's silver shoe, a sign of great foreboding to his people. He did fight at Killiecrankie but, unlike Sir Ewen, did not play a noticeable part. Nonetheless it was John who commanded the clan after his father returned to Lochaber following the Jacobites' eventual defeat.

Some three years previously, in 1696, Sir Ewen had made over the family estates in Lochaber to John so that, in 1706, when a warrant was issued for his apprehension on the charge of treason incurred by rising in arms against King William at the Battle of Killiecrankie in 1689, John handed over all his lands to Donald, his eldest son, then a boy of only six years old.

John remained at Achnacarry for another eleven years, the threat of arrest prorogued. During this time a fifth son, named Euan, was born. It was accepted that, as in most Highland families, while Donald as the eldest would become chief of the clan, his four younger brothers would have to make their own way in the world. But it was the youngest brother Euan who, when he became a planter in Jamaica on the estate bought there by his grandfather Sir Ewen, with great foresight recognized the value of the sugar that could be grown there. He was not alone in his speculation. Other families in the west of Scotland were sending their cadet members to make fortunes in the Caribbean islands where, if not killed by diseases such as yellow fever, huge profits could be made.

There were three other children in addition to the five boys. One, a daughter named Peggy, died young, as did two other children of whom nothing is known.

John Cameron, unlike his father, had no longing for war. A peaceable man, he was more interested in trying to increase the income of the family's estates. Locked in dispute, like his forefathers, over the validity of conflicting charter rights of their territories with the Mackintoshes and other neighbouring clans, he tried to effect security with a solidly loyal Cameron tenantry. Imbued with the right of jurisdiction as were all Highland chiefs at that time, his tenants and their dependents accepted his right to settle, not only their rights to territory under his suzerainty, but all cases of assault and robbery down to the smallest degree.

Above all he was faced with problems raised by increasing population, as due to advancing medical knowledge more children survived. His attempts to increase production from the small stretches of arable land certainly inspired his eldest son. While his business acumen was passed on to John, his second son, it is reasonable to think that it was his humane outlook which set the seeds of serving their fellows in the minds of the next two boys who followed in age. Alexander, a particularly lively and attractive lad, who was destined to turn to religion and Archie, quieter and less exuberant, who would serve his fellow countrymen in a necessary but different way.

The children enjoyed freedom such as many would envy today. Unsupervised they learnt to be self-reliant in the wild stretch of country which was theirs to explore.

As then was common in the Highlands, Alexander was fostered by the Camerons of Glendessary, a place not far from Achnacarry to which he frequently returned. Perhaps in reaction to the strictness of his own upbringing under a tyrannical father, John is known to have been a particularly affectionate parent, as indeed was Isobel, his wife. Closely involved as he was with his young family it must have been with great reluctance that he led his clan to fight for the exiled King James, the Roman Catholic son of James II, when summoned by the Earl of Mar.

The handover of the Lochiel estates by John to his eldest son Donald proved to be a wise precaution. John Cameron was a committed Jacobite who took part in all the political intrigues of the Highland chiefs which culminated in the Rising of 1715. At the root of it all was the problem over the succession. Queen Anne herself is believed to have wished that her half-brother James, the Chevalier de St George, as he was known, would follow her rather than her distant cousin the Elector of Hanover.

Many people in Scotland felt the same. A Stuart monarch had ruled the English for barely more than a century, but the Scots, since the succession of Bruce's grandson, Robert the Steward, had been ruled by them for nearly four hundred years.

But during that time, in 1560, the Reformation had taken place. Presbyterianism was now the dominant creed, centred on the Scottish Kirk and James VII & II had been forced to flee Great Britain because of his Roman Catholic faith. Now, for the same reason, the majority of people in the parliament were against the return of his son. Families were divided in their loyalties and foremost for the acceptance of the Elector of Hanover was John, Duke of Argyll.

Not all of his clan agreed with him. John, Earl of Breadalbane, whom John Cameron noted had been most supportive to James, although too old to take the field, sent a deputy to fight on his behalf. Campbell of Auchinbreck, father of Donald Cameron's wife Anne, a convert to Catholicism, his land in Knapdale stretching from coast to coast, called out his men to fight for James. The country was in a ferment of disagreement over contrasting loyalties, rumours of rebellion foremost in almost every mind.

On 18th October 1710, the Elector of Bavaria's minister at Versailles sent a dispatch to tell him that:

> The Duke of Berwick who was informed a good while ago, that this chance would be made, wrote to Monsieur de Torey, to represent to the King *(Louis XV)* that this would be the right time to attempt a descent, not in Scotland, but in England; and that he would gladly put himself at the head of twenty thousand men to carry the King of England *(The Chevalier)* thither with certain success.
>
> Thus the plan was laid by that ministry for the introduction of the Pretender. And with that view they clapt the famous Peace of Utrecht, to gratify their Patron, the King of France, by whose alliance the change was to be brought about...
>
> The Queen's health being at last dispair'd of, the friends of the House of Hanover, thought it high time to take measures to prevent the machinations of the Ministry on so critical a conjecture. Accordingly the Dukes of Argyle and Somerset went, without being summoned, to the Grand Chamber at Kensington where the chief ministers were met in a committee to deliberate on the manner of proclaiming the Pretender on the event of the Queen's death.[6]

'Red John of the Battles', John 2nd Duke of Argyll, was a man not to be trifled with. Neither was Algernon Seymour, 7th Duke of Somerset, both being used to command. Staunch Protestants and Whigs they opposed the innovation of a Roman Catholic monarch. Forcing their way into the chamber the two dominated the assembly, demanding that all Privy Councillors then in and about London should be summoned immediately, thus insuring that supporters for the Protestant Elector should win the day. Consequently, when Queen Anne died on 1st August 1714, the Elector became King George I.

According to the same source; '*The party for the Pretender appeared thunderstruck, their surprise to see all their fine scheme baffled in a minute was so great that it was some time before they could recover* (from) *their astonishment'.* But they soon began plotting again. Meanwhile collections were made for the 'Pretender' as he became commonly known, in all the Roman Catholic countries throughout Europe.[7]

Tension increased as John, Earl of Mar, slighted when George I turned his back on him at a levy, became leader of his opponents, the Jacobites as they were termed. When Mar raised his standard at Braemar the Rising of 1715 began.

John Cameron was ordered to lead the clan by his father Sir Ewen, by then too old to take the field. In a long letter to the chieftains of Clan Cameron he gave his own account of what happened at the Battle of Sheriffmuir. Following a council of war:

> We agreed to fight and to march along the skirt of the Sheriff moor till we came above the enemie. In the meantime my Lord Marrishall was ordered with his squadron to attack a part of ye enemy's horse which appeared on the top of the hill...and at the same time the whole army to begin our march, we were then ordered into four columns. How soon the Earl Marrishall came

> close upon the enemie's horse, which we saw on the hill, he perceived Argyle's whole army on their march up ye hill; of which he immediately acquaints my Lord Mar, upon which our whole army marched up in very great haste, which occasioned some confusion, tho never men marched with greater cheerfulness towards ane enemy.[8]

A confused, incomplete deployment into the line of battle followed. The men of a Lowland Jacobite regiment on the left wing broke rank and ran under Hanoverian fire carrying the Camerons with them as they fled. John Cameron had gone a little way ahead to reconnoitre and could only stand and watch in horror the debacle that was taking place, *'which was my fate'.*

John, with two or three others, then crossed the River Allan where he met Rob Roy Macgregor with about two hundred and fifty men. Rob Roy, however, refused point blank to re-cross the river to attack Argyll. With night coming on Cameron managed to reach a little village above Braco, where he got a message from Mar to join him at Auchterarder the next day. From there the army marched to Perth where King James, on his arrival, ordered Cameron *'to goe home to ye Highlands'* to raise his own men and those of the neighbouring clans. John first went to Taymouth where he saw Lord Breadalbane, *'who was very earnest I would raise his men in Lorn, and to march them to the army with the rest of my command'.*[9]

Struggling through deep snow-drifts he managed to reach Lochaber but dared not stay at Achnacarry because the garrison at Inverlochy was so close by. Afterwards *'oblig'd to lurke up and down the contry of Lochabar'* he at last went to hide in Sunart and Morvern, but search parties were soon on his trail.

Returning secretly to Lochaber to try to settle his affairs before leaving the country, he found Achnacarry occupied by soldiers who were *'destroying and plundering all they could seize of my effects of all kinds'.* Told that a company of the forces looking for him was only a mile away, he somehow managed to get to the Isle of Skye where, finding his brother Allan, they went on together to Uist.

There, on 24th June 1716, he wrote the letter to the principal men of his clan telling them that:

> Since by the present posture of my affairs, my continuing with you cannot advance the King my master's service, nor our Country's nor contribute in the least to your safety or my own, obliges me to leave you so abruptly, and take this occasion, with some other worthy persons, to follow my prince.[10]

Thus did John Cameron explain his reasons for leaving Scotland before sailing shortly for France.

Chapter 3
SONS WITHOUT A FATHER

John's explanation for the military disaster at Sheriffmuir was not accepted. 'Not the same man as his father', the stigma would pursue him to his death.

Yet his forward thinking on land improvement remained imbued in the minds of his sons. Particularly he envisaged a great future in cattle raising rather than stealing them from neighbouring clans, so long a reason for protracted feuds. John, had he stayed in Scotland, would have been an improving laird. Exiled, tainted a traitor, he had to leave his plans for land development to be carried out by his sons.

Tantalizingly, in his letter he makes no mention of either them or his wife. When he writes that *'his house was occupied by government soldiers'* he presumably means Achnacarry. If so the question arises of what became of his family. Possibly, indeed probably, they remained in Achnacarry with only an armed guard, the members of which being only too happy to enjoy some warmth and well-cooked food.

Certainly it is known that the five boys, Donald, John, Alexander, Archibald, always known as Archie, and Euan grew up at Achnacarry in the traditional ways of the Highlands. Wearing the kilt and plaid, a garment then made in the old-fashioned way in one piece, they went barefoot in the summer, shoes being only permissible with the first coming of snow. They learnt how to ride and break horses, to fish in the rivers and lochs, and to shoot with a fusil, as the old firelocks were known. Also, of greatest importance, they were taught how to use a sword, the weapon, strapped to his side, without which a Highland gentleman could never be seen alive. In addition he carried a dirk and, in the presence of danger, a pistol and a powder horn as well.

While the great gatherings of Sir Ewen's day had passed visitors, mostly relations and septs of the Clan, came to stay. Among them were his daughter Isobel and her husband, Archibald Cameron of Dungallon, from Sunart, who came with their three sons and three daughters to make long visits during the summer months. Amongst the girls Jean was the prettiest, at least in the eyes of young Archie, who vied for her attention with his three older brothers, more dashing and sophisticated than himself.

Few of the young Camerons, competitive as they may have been with each other, were aware of the ever growing anger of that other family, the Camerons of Glennevis, living below the massive mountain of Ben Nevis. Most fervent in his resentment was Samuel, one of Glennevis's younger sons, born with a deformity of his legs and dubbed 'Crookshanks' from his youngest days. Aware of his being compared by the local people to the Lochiel boys, all of them straight-limbed and handsome, Samuel knew himself an outcast, a misfit from the moment of his birth.

Chapter 4
THE STUDENTS

Shortly after their father's exile, Alexander was sent to boarding school at St Ninian's near Stirling, the fees being paid by his foster father, Cameron of Glendessary.

Monsignor Thomas Wynne, in his biography of Alexander, believes that both Archie and Euan went with him, but Andrew Henderson, Archie's contemporary biographer, says that he received his early education from a Mr Alexander MacBaine, Minister of Inverness, *'a very honest man, and my particular friend'.*[11]

To get to Inverness he probably went by boat up Loch Ness, this being the most common form of transport in the Highlands, the military road on the south shore of the loch being as yet unmade. With him, no doubt, went a servant, wrapped like himself in a plaid against the wind blowing down the Loch. His luggage included a bag of oatmeal with which to make his porridge at wherever it was that he would stay in the town.

Under MacBaine he was initiated into the principles of the Latin and Greek tongues then, as Henderson says, *'the Principal Part of education in Scotland at that time':*

> And as Mr MacBaine understood these Languages well, and had an acute Genius to work upon, Mr Cameron became a good Proficient in these studies, and was afterwards sent to the College of Glasgow, where he improved his Latin under Mr Andrew Ross, a Man of great Knowledge in the Latin Tongue, being a Person of a quick Turn of Mind, but without any solid Judgement.[12]

Henderson added in a footnote that Ross subsequently died mad.

Archie also improved his knowledge of ancient Greek under a Mister Dunlop, author of a book on grammar in which:

> he reduces the declentions to three, marking down the active, passive, and middle voice, both of the regular and irregular verbs so anyone who knew the alphabet could learn Greek on his own.

He likewise studied moral philosophy under Mr Francis Hutchinson, an Irishman *'who wrote with great elegance on the passions and moral virtue'*. He learned some parts of what Henderson called *'the Mathematicks'* from Mr Robert Simpson, *'who has wrote a most elaborate and excellent Treatise of Conic Sections, and at his Leisure Hours heard Lectures from Mr John Simpson, the Professor of Divinity'.*[13]

This was the man who through the malice of some of the students at the university had been traduced and labelled as the Enemy to the Divinity of Jesus Christ. Manipulated by Lord Grange, brother of the Earl of Mar, who wanted to divide the Kirk, poor Mr Simpson had been victimized to the point where he had been tortured for several years. Released at last, a hero to his supporters, he was once more allowed to resume his lectures on divinity.

John Cameron wrote from France urging Archie to study for the Scottish bar. However, on Archie himself becoming convinced of the duplicity of lawyers, discovering that *'in order to be properly qualified for an advocate he must be master of all the quirks and sophistical reasonings, that are usually made use of to puzzle a cause and to hoodwink the understanding with factitious argument'* he abandoned that project and decided to become a doctor'.[14] His father accepted his decision. But his eldest brother Donald, now in charge of things at home, was less than confident of his choice:

> My brother Archie has capacity enough but no application, he learned his logic, but I am afraid to little purpose, he has made no great advance in his Greek or Latin, and it will be to no purpose to send him *(letter torn)* especially since his brother can't continue with him. He's inclined to be a doctor, which you know, without being master of Greek or Latin he cannot propose to follow, besides the vast expense I must be at, which my circumstances cannot bear, so that, in my opinion, to bind him prentice to an able surgeon is the best way to dispose of him, and what little stock he has himself, with a little addition, may pay his prentice fee.[15]

From this it would seem that Archie had run through most of the money gifted to him by his father before he left for France. Possibly some of it had disappeared in the Glasgow taverns, it being hard to believe that a young man of his age spent all his spare time listening to the good Mr Simpson, Professor of Divinity, however eloquent his lectures.

Somehow he must have got round Donald, or some other member of his family, possibly his mother, to help him, for shortly he left Glasgow for Edinburgh University. There he applied to study Anatomy under Doctor Alexander Munro, founder of the Edinburgh Medical School, who had become Professor of Anatomy at Edinburgh University at the age of twenty-one. Likewise, according to his biographer Henderson, he studied physics under Doctor Sinclair, better known as St Clair, one of the most eminent professors of his day.

Munro had himself studied in Paris, where he had performed operations under the direction of Thibaut and had instruction in midwifery from Gregoire. For the purpose of explaining and illustrating the different stages of pregnancy, he kept foetuses in glass jars for his students to study, thus giving them practical knowledge that could not be obtained in any other way.

Later Archie Cameron would come to be regarded with the respect due to a wizard as he saved the lives of women enduring difficult deliveries, and those of otherwise maimed or still born infants in remote Highland glens.

More factually, in a list of students who studied medicine in Edinburgh, Archie is recorded as a student of John Blair, a fellow of the Royal College of Surgeons in Edinburgh in 1723, for which year he paid an honorarium of three guineas. Again in a list dated 18th October 1727, he paid another three guineas to the same John Blair, while in a third list, dated 12th January 1728, he paid one guinea, once again to John Blair.[16]

Some time in 1726, while Archie was studying in Edinburgh, he was joined by his elder brother Alexander, their younger brother Euan having already left for Jamaica where he was to spend the rest of his life. Alexander was funded by the sale of the thirty cows gifted to him by his foster father at Glendessary, amounting to over £150. He also had a Bond of Provision gifted by his father, amounting to 8,000 merks. (a merk is an old Scots coin equalling 13 shillings and 4 pence). Euan had been given 6,000 merks so presumably Archie had received about the same.

Leaving Scotland Archie travelled to Paris. The journey was comparatively easy at a time when all travel was hazardous. Ships went back and forth regularly to Flanders from the east coast ports across the North Sea, their holds filled with Scottish goods such as salmon on the outward voyage, and with cargoes, often of the wine then drunk so copiously in Scotland, on the return. From the Netherlands it was easy to continue to France, hiring horses at Post Houses on roads constructed long before anything similar had been built beyond the Highland line.

The men under whom Archie studied in Paris remain unnamed. All that is known for certain is that here he was united with his father who, given a commission in the French army, was receiving a pension from the King. The joy of their reunion can only be imagined. John was thirsting to know of the welfare of his family and of how things were at Achnacarry, the home to which he could not return.

It is not known whether John's wife Isobel left Achnacarry to join him in exile in Paris. Many Jacobite wives did so, but Isobel may not have felt up to making the journey, or to leaving all that was familiar, perhaps on account of her health. The affection shown to him by his sons, however, is evident from the visits that three of them made to him over a number of years. Donald had already been to Paris and would come again. John, by now a man of business, is not known to have gone to France, but Alexander, who had been to visit his brother Euan in Jamaica and travelled round the Caribbean, came to see him much at the same time as Archie who, if he did a course of lectures, must have stayed for a period of several months.

It is also possible that Archie spent some time in the medieval town of Leyden, in Flanders, birthplace of Rembrandt and seat of the oldest University in Holland. Founded in 1575 to commemorate the resistance of the townsfolk to a Spanish siege, it had since gained a reputation as the European centre for the study of both medicine and law.

The assumption of Archie being there is based on the fact that Munro himself had been a pupil under Professor Boerhaave, to whom came students from far and wide. Amongst them were many Scots who, in Munro's time, had been placed under his care.

Wherever he finished his training, Archie is known to have become fully qualified as a doctor. It is also claimed that his father begged him to stay in France. But, whatever the disappointment that this must have caused to his parent, Archie remained determined to go back to Scotland, as had been always his intent.

Chapter 5
LOYALTY AND WAR

Archie Cameron had his own good reasons for wanting to return home. He had long courted his cousin, Jean Cameron of Dungallon, the girl with whom on her visits with her family to Achnacarry he had fallen in love. His wooing was made more difficult by the fact that her family lived in Glenhurich, in Sunart, about thirty miles as the crow flies from Achnacarry.

In those days this was a day's journey either on horseback or on foot, possibly going some of the way by boat. But young men in the Highlands frequently walked long distances of fifty miles or more and Archie was fit and strong. Determined to marry her, he asked her father for her hand, a request that was gladly given due to the friendship between the families, although Archie, without great prospects, was only a younger son.

He did, however, have some property, for on his marriage, or shortly afterwards, his brother Donald gave him the tack (lease held on a military basis) of Glen Kingie. The tack, almost certainly, would have included a tacksman's house which, stone built with lyme and roofed with slate, was superior to the cottars' simple rough stone dwellings covered with heather or turf.

The River Kingie, rising in the mountains to the north of Loch Arkaig, runs from the high ground down to a green strath before it joins the River Garry. Accessible only by a track, even in the present day, it seems unlikely that Archie and his young family lived there in the winter months. Known to have moved from place to place, sometimes tending the sick in Morvern, sometimes in Glendessary, he plainly had a peripatetic life.[17]

Whatever the vagueness of his actual whereabouts, one thing that is certain, from every contemporary account, is that Doctor Archie played a major part in helping his brother Donald to civilize the men and even the women of their clan.

In the Highlands of Scotland, where cattle lifting had long been accepted as a way of making a living in a bare countryside, the Camerons had long been known as the greatest reivers of them all. The full moon was dubbed 'Lochiel's Lantern' because so many cattle were stolen under its pale light. Donald was to earn the name of the 'Gentle Lochiel' largely because he forbade this practice, much to his clansmen's dismay. Alexander Henderson, in a eulogy, wrote:

> When the late Donald Cameron of Lochiel came to the estate, he found himself at the head of a very potent clan, which laboured under the imputation of pilfery and robbery, to extirpate which two detestable vices, he applied himself with the utmost vigour and in the course of his procedure exerted uncommon labour and pains. No person reputed to have stole a cow, a sheep, or a horse, was ever admitted into his presence, and he gave the reward of his countenance to those who were most instrumental in detecting robbery and theft, the few strangers who came among them (for every person is a stranger in these Highland counties, except themselves) were regaled by him, and publick intimation was made that his example should be followed. And indeed his endeavours were crowned with such success, that before the breaking out of the last uprising, he himself was looked upon as the most polite gentleman in the Highlands, and his clan the most civilized. Nor must it be forgot that his brother, the unfortunate subject of these memoirs, was singularly active in promoting these salutary schemes, which argued the greater virtue, if we consider that at this time the clan were under the influence of Lovat, as will easily appear from the following story, which is known to some gentlemen of great veracity,

with whom I conversed about it not many days since.[18]

He then proceeded to relate a most revolting story of how *'Simon Lord Lovat, whose name has made such a noise in the world'*, revenged himself on a Mr Cuthbert of Castlehill who, acting as umpire, had decided in favour of the neighbour with whom Lovat had been in dispute. Lovat's letter to Ludovic Cameron, Lochiel and Archie's uncle, if not exactly relevant to a biography of the latter, provides nonetheless a classic example of the hypocrisy and double dealing of a fellow chief with whom they had to contend:

> My dear cousin Mr Ludovick Cameron
>
> This comes by an express to inform you, that your dear cousin and faithful servant Simon Lord Lovat, is in great distress in both body and mind; not so much for the loss I have of late sustained through the determination and arbitriment of Cuthbert of Castlehill, as from that rages in my breast to see the Boddach Sassanachs, daily encroaching upon the clans...my very heart is about to burst within me when I think upon the losses sustained by the clans, who are dearer to me than my very life, and what heightens my pain is to think that you should have your ears wracked, and eyes polluted, with reading this account, which I am obliged to send you, for sure I am, my dear cousin, that if your honest grandfather, who bit the Boddach Sassanach's lip, for which and other services he was knighted by my dear master King Charles II was alive, his very heart would break within him, for no people upon earth were more intimate than he and I. And now I beg leave, my dear cousin, to inform you what he once did for my father. A Boddach Sassanach once differed with my father and on his telling his complaint to my dear cousin, your grandfather, he sent his own brother to revenge

> the quarrel, for in two days time all his stables were broken, and his horses and cattle driven into the sea...And now, my dear cousin, if some speedy remedy be not applied, these Boddach Sassanachs will triumph over us, which you can easily prevent, so that I shall be in pain till I hear of and from my dear cousin.[19]

This letter, extraordinary as it may seem, spurred Ludovic Cameron into action, for three days after he had received it all the cows in the Parks of Castlehill were houghed, or hamstrung. Two men ordered to be hanged and promised a reprieve by Lovat, only realized that he had double-crossed them as the ropes were being put round their necks, *'Such was the genius of the people of Lochaber, when the late Donald Cameron of Lochiel came to the estate'* continued Henderson:

> and like another Peter the Great of Muscovy, not only applied to polishing his own people in good earnest, but set a bright and laudable example to his neighbours of Glengarry and Keppoch, the MacPhersons and Grants, whose clans were more thieves and cruel than even the Camerons themselves. His brother, Doctor Archibald, relished the undertaking, and being naturally of a very mild, amiable disposition and of the sweetest temper of mind, his councils were the more persuasive, and his endeavours more successful.[20]

Donald, in fact, had the acumen to realize that, under the present conditions, the old ways must necessarily change. He could not guess, nor could anyone else, except perhaps for a few clear sighted minds, that the Highlands and Islands of Scotland were on the cusp of a transformation that would lead to the end of the centuries old organization of clan society as it stood. Had he foreseen the coming changes he might, at least in some ways, have felt a sense of relief.

Lochiel, who had married Anne, daughter of Sir James Campbell of Auchinbreck, an eccentric who was commonly in debt, had to provide not only for his own family of three boys and four girls, but for the many indigent families on his wide estates, on an income drawn from the rents of only £700 a year.

The responsibility thrust upon him from such a very young age was certainly taking its toll. As the clan chief he was looked upon not only as the patriarchal leader but the provider in times of want, an only too common occurrence in a country where, thanks to the poor soil and the climate, (Lochaber has one of the highest rainfalls in Scotland) the harvest frequently failed. In these years he had to import grain from Glasgow or wherever it could be found, to be landed at Fort William. Inevitably, in times of shortage, the merchants then raised their prices which, thanks to the poverty of his tenants, he had to bear himself.

The financial situation was eased in 1735 when he sold Fassifern, on the north side of Loch Eil, to his brother John, a successful trader and a burgess of Glasgow. Because of this, the last thing that Donald looked for was involvement in plans for another rising to restore the exiled king.

Chapter 6
THE DEVIL'S CHOICE

Some ten years before, on 11th April 1725, King James VIII, as he was known in Scotland, had written to Lochiel from Rome. Addressing him as 'Mr Johnstone, junior', the pseudonym he used as part of a code, he told him:

> I am glad of this occasion to let you know how well pleased I am of the care you take to follow your father's and uncle's example in their loyalty to me; and I doubt not of your endeavour to maintain the true spirit of the clan. Allan *(uncle of Donald and Archie)* is now with me, and I am always glad to have some of my brave Highlanders about me, whom I value as they deserve. You will deliver the enclosed to its address, and doubt not of my particular regard for you, which I am persuaded you will always deserve.
>
> (signed) James R.[21]

The implication was obvious. The King did intend to make another attempt to overthrow the Hanoverian monarch, if not immediately then at some future date. Meanwhile Lochiel must keep the fires of revolution burning in Scotland. It was plainly and simply an order, not merely a request.

As far as is known Donald did not reply to the letter. He was unwilling to commit himself to what he knew would be disastrous for the country.

Fourteen years had passed since James's own failed rising of 1715, and ten following the attempted invasion from Spain by the Earl Marischal in 1719. Scotland was only just recovering, both in human terms, and financially, from the ruination of civil war. Now, however, on 11th September 1729, Lochiel eventually wrote to his uncle, Allan Cameron, mentioned by the King in his letter as being by his side.

Allan Cameron, the third son of Sir Ewen, described as *'a man of extraordinary parts and great integrity'* was he who had landed with King James at Peterhead in December 1715, as seen by his father in a dream. Having recently been in Scotland to confer with the Highland chiefs, he had just returned to Albano, from where he replied to his nephew, telling him he had shown his letter to the King:

> who not only was pleased to say that you wrote with a great deal of Zeal and common sense, but was so gracious and good as to write you a letter with his own hand, herewith sent you, wherein he gives full and ample powers to treat with such of his friends in Scotland, as you think are safe to be trusted in what concerns his affairs, until an opportunity offers for executing any reasonable project towards a happy restoration, which they cannot expect to know until matters be entirely ripe for execution, and of which they will be acquainted directly from himself.[22]

In this letter to Donald of several pages, Allan continued:

> the King, as well as Mr Hay, did me assure that your father should never be in any more straits, as long as he, the King, lived; and that he would take care from time to time to remit him; so that I hope you may be pretty easy as to that point.

He then proceeded to give him some advice, evidently dictated by the King at the instigation of Old Lochiel, as Donald's exiled father was known. Referring to the long-standing feud between the Camerons and the MacDonells of Glengarry, he told him:

> You are to keep on good terms with Glengarry, and all other neighbours and let bygones be bygones, as long as they continue firm to the King's interest; let no private animosity take place, but see to gain them with courtesy and good management, which I hope will give you an opportunity to make a figure amongst them, not but you are to tell the truth, if any of them fail in their duty to the King or country.

These words have a sinister undertone in the event of what was to come. What did the King know about past feuds with the neighbours, particularly with Glengarry, a man known to have been a sadist who cruelly treated his wife?

While his mistrust of Lovat is understandable, his devious character being well known, his reference to the other chiefs, Glengarry in particular, must refer to the ongoing dissention which had existed between the two clans since Glengarry's desertion of Sir Ewen at Aberchalder during Glencairn's Rising. Allan recognized Glengarry as a threat but his nephew, Doctor Archie, unsuspecting to the point of being gullible, if he read the letter to his brother, did not take the warning on board.

Finally, there being no better person to do so than himself, married as he was to his daughter, he advised him on how to deal with Lord Lovat:

> As to Lovat, pray be always on your guard, but not so as to lose him; on the contrary, you may say that the King trusts a great deal to the resolution he has taken to serve him; and expects he will continue in that resolution. But, dear nephew, you know very well that he must give true and real proof of his sincerity, by performance, before he can be entirely reckoned on, after the part he has acted. This I say to yourself; and therefore you must deal with him very dexterously; and I must leave it to your

own judgement what lengths to go with him, since you know he has always been a man whose chief view was his own interest. It is true he wishes our family well; and I doubt he would wish the King restored, which is his interest, if he has the grace to have a hand in it after what he has done. So, upon the whole, I know not what advice to give you, as to letting him know what the King wrote you such a letter as you have; but in general you are to make the best of him you can, but still be on your guard, for it is not good to put too much in his power before the time of executing a good design, The King knows very well how useful he can be if sincere, which I have represented as fully as was necessary.[23]

Chapter 7
THE NEW ROADS

Captain Burt of the army engineers, in his *Letters from a Gentleman in the North of Scotland to His Friend in London,* described a country without roads. Tracks over the hills were dangerous: peat bogs a hidden menace to the traveller. There were few if any bridges so that fords were extremely hazardous in time of heavy rain. Ferry crossings likewise were perilous, the boats being leaky and so small that horses had to swim behind. Snowdrifts could block off the glens, sometimes for months at a time. The inns were primitive, the food often so badly cooked as to be inedible. Plainly the captain was unimpressed to say the least.

Lochiel was amongst the landlords who envisaged the benefits that the building of the military roads would bring to the country. In the early 1730s a new military road was being constructed under the direction of General Wade, from Crieff across the Grampians to Inverness. Already a road up the Great Glen linked Fort William to Inverness, from where a branch was then taken down the upper reaches of the Spey and over the Corrieyairack Pass to the newly built Fort Augustus.

The sight of General Wade, driving up from his home in Bath in a coach drawn by six horses, was one of the great excitements to people in the Highlands who had never before seen such an equipage. A genial man, a generous host, he is known to have spent convivial evenings with the local lairds who must have included many of the Camerons in the area around Fort William.

A contemporary description of how both Lochiel and his brother Doctor Archie gave assistance to Wade's road building emphasizes that *'they laid the strictest commands on the whole of their men, to be obliging to the soldiers, and to do everything in their power to rendering the situation agreeable so that whatever misrepresentations Mr Wade might give of Scotland, he had no reason to complain'.*[24]

Whether or not Doctor Archie attended to the soldiers in a medical capacity is not specified, but it is known that Lochiel supplied both beef and venison for the garrison, much to the General's satisfaction.

As the days grew shorter and the geese overhead flew south, preparations were made to stave off hunger, which in the months before the next harvest must inevitably occur. Deer were culled in early autumn when, after feeding on summer grass, their meat was most tender. Men, boys and barking dogs chased them from the hills into narrow gullies, where marksmen with long bored rifles, Lochiel himself and Doctor Archie amongst them, shot enough beasts to fill the tubs in which salted meat kept families from starvation.

Such was the time-honoured practice, but in the Highlands of the mid-18th century, as elsewhere in Scotland, agricultural improvements were becoming the talk of the day. The age old methods of farming continued, as cattle were driven in summer to graze on the hills so that crops could be grown on the strips of arable ground in the glens below. Traditionally, most of the cattle were killed before Christmas, fodder being so scarce. But as they became more valuable, thanks to trade with England, more were being driven to the markets to be sold on the hoof. This proved an added reason why the traditional habit of cattle reiving had to be brought to a stop. Donald Lochiel was one who forbade it on threat of punishment to the miscreants.

Remembered as he is today for his determination to subdue the often barbarous behaviour of his people, the participation of his brother Archie in what seems to have amounted to a campaign to reform the lawless behaviour of the people of Lochaber, has largely faded into obscurity.

Chapter 8
THE GENERAL PRACTITIONER

Andrew Henderson, Doctor Archie's contemporary biographer, left a full description of what life was like for a practitioner in the Highlands of Scotland in those days:

> He practised physic in these remote parts, where, by a genteel behaviour, and by countenancing honesty and industry, he was very instrumental in reforming these poor people, hitherto so gross in their morals, that theft was the very characteristic and signature by which they were known.[25]

Burt gives a humorous description of a clan chief accompanied on his travels by his retinue, known as his fiery tail, and his ghillies, one carrying his broadsword, and another taking him over the fords, because a chief wore tartan trews rather than a kilted plaid. Doctor Archie, however, even if wearing trews, more practical for riding astride, would certainly have wrapped himself in a plaid for warmth on the journeys over the moors and mountains which he so frequently made.

As a young man Archie Cameron must have been physically strong. In a practice stretching from Loch Arkaig to the south end of Sunart, an area of about twenty-five square miles, he had long distances to travel in all weathers, in every season of the year and, as with other doctors in remote country places, he was summoned at all hours of the day and night.

Although riding himself on a strong Highland garron (pony), his medical bag strapped to the saddle, it is likely that he took with him a ghillie who, walking ahead in the darkness and showing the path by a covered lantern, led the way to remote cottages in the hills.

He was always close to danger, particularly during the winter months. Sudden spates could cause land-slides, carrying away narrow paths. A false step could mean a plunge into a void below. Burt did not exaggerate the hazard of crossing fords, where currents could drag a man from his horse or sweep animals off their feet.

Archie was much loved by the local people as Henderson avers. Thanks to his knowledge of obstetrics, both women, who so often died in childbirth, and also their babies were saved by his skill. To the local people, to whom he spoke in their own Gaelic tongue, Doctor Archie became an oracle, a man possessed of superhuman knowledge, in whom they had implicit faith.

His patients must have welcomed him, not only as a doctor, but as a man bringing news of the outside world. Many of these Gaelic-speaking people, except on the rarest occasions, never left their homes in the remote glens. That is not to say they were lonely, for most had neighbours with whom to spend the winter evenings sitting round a peat fire. The majority of houses had a bible in which were kept records of the births, marriages and deaths of the family concerned. Captain Burt, while noticing what, to his English eyes, was *'their wretched poverty, itching skins, and faces darkened by the smoke of their hovels'*, was nonetheless impressed by the people's intense pride in the history of their family and clan.

At that time, before so much of the land was given over to sheep runs, the rents being low all arable ground was cultivated with oats as the main crop. Main tenants, or tacksmen, rented the farms on a basis involving military commitment while their sub tenants, or cottars, who actually worked the ground, had a few cows of their own. Beyond the cultivated areas grazing was communal, every tenant having cattle in proportion to his rent. There were also a few sheep and goats.

Tradesmen, including stone masons, tailors and shoemakers, lived and worked in the farming townships. The older generation was mostly illiterate but children, in the less distant places walked, sometimes over many miles, to the few Parish Schools or to those set up by the S.P.C.K, (the Society for the Promotion of Christian Knowledge).

The average wage for a schoolmaster was then about £9 to £12 per annum, to which was added the perquisite of keeping a cow. Living however was cheap, a pound of beef or mutton costing just over a penny, a goose one or two pence, a hen two pence. Herrings salted in a barrel were a mainstay of many poor people.

The houses were very primitive, inside sanitation being hardly heard of in the Highlands at that time. Most were of the traditional 'but and ben', two rooms divided by a small closet in which the dairy dishes were kept. Some of the poorer cottages, however, consisted of only a single room.

Inevitably, as the birth rate rose, making families of six or seven, or even more children no uncommon thing, such overcrowded conditions increased the spread of disease. Diphtheria was particularly deadly, as were the outbreaks of smallpox which all too frequently occurred. Parish registers also show deaths from tetanus, another main killer in agricultural communities, the presence of deadly bacteria in the soil being as yet unknown.

The local people, unused to any so-called medical cures, tended to cling to the herbal remedies handed down through generations to cure ills. A distillation of the little plant eyebright, for instance, being used for eye infections, and sphagnum moss to prevent gangrene in wounds.

Doctor Archie, the only medical practitioner in Sunart and Lochaber, may initially have had to overcome opposition to modern methods as he treated his patients with the few known medicines of his time.

Almost certainly his own dispenser, he perhaps employed a boy to rub down the ingredients with a pestle and mortar; rhubarb, ground down into pills, being the common panacea of his day. Calomel, a white powder, was used for constipation, while nitric acid, greatly diluted in water, was a palliative for both sickness and ulcers. Rheumatism, due to the poor housing conditions and wet weather, was the main complaint, almost impossible to alleviate in those times. An extract of willow bark was used to relieve pain as opium, imported by the British East India Company from China was not only very expensive but, in places as remote as the Highlands, not yet in common use. Poultices, coated with mustard, were the cure for a variety of ills. Poor as they were most people could not pay him in money, so it was usually something in kind, a chicken, a slab of butter, half a dozen eggs or some bannocks, there was always something for the doctor to take away, as well as their heartfelt thanks.

It was not a lucrative practice but Archie and Jean Cameron, like so many people in the district, got an income from their herd of cattle, as their dealing in the animals was soon to show. Lochiel had 6,000 black cattle of his own. He had given the tack of Glen Kingie to his brother – Archie was known as Doctor Archibald Cameron of Glenkingie – specifically to allow him to make a living through farming above that of a country practitioner dependent on gifts from people with hardly a penny to their names.

It was now nearly forty years since the Act of Union had opened the English markets to Scottish trade. Sales of the small black and brown Highland cattle had grown steadily as people south of the border realized the excellence of Scottish beef. Then, in 1742, at the onset of the War of the Austrian Succession, the government needed salted meat to feed both the army and the navy. The price of cattle increased to the point where over 20,000 animals were being sold annually at Crieff.[26] The boom had begun.

Highland gentlemen, from the chiefs down to their lowest tenants, realized there was money to be made on land that had hitherto yielded nothing except grouse and deer and the few beasts killed in late autumn for the pot. The cattle trade brought employment; Archie Cameron needed men to herd his cattle in Glen Kingie whose families were his patients, and these herdsmen had a few cattle of their own which were sold by the drovers, who took them down to the market and came back with the money in their sporrans. They were trusted men, honest to the last penny, as were most people in the Highlands of that time in dealings amongst themselves.

The profitable trade in cattle had a downside, for the beef tubs were less full than in former days. The mainstay of most families being oatmeal, people lacking protein became anaemic. Doctor Archie urged them to grow cabbages in the kail yards most cottagers shared. But Highland people, steeped in tradition, were stubborn, slow even at sight of their children's pale faces to change their ways. Even forty years later there was not a turnip in Ardnamurchan of which Sunart is a part.

The fact that Doctor Archie was described as itinerant *'sometimes tending the sick in Morvern, sometimes at Glendessary,*[27] suggests that he was frequently away from home. If with his family he did live in Glen Kingie it can only have been for a short time until they found the house in Strontian of which there is documentary proof. They may, however, have gone to Glen Kingie in the late summer to help bring in the hay harvest and the corn.

In those days in the Highlands crops were so vital to survival that everyone gave a hand to bring them in. Women hitched up their skirts to make stooks of the corn scythed by the men, while children, running barefoot, raked up the loose grass.

That Archie and Jean did not live permanently in the glen from which they took their name is shown by an anonymous document, written in pencil, which states that *'his residence in Strontian was called Batchelor's Hall'.*

=============

In 1722 Sir Alexander Murray discovered galena, the natural mineral form of lead, in the hills of Sunart. A mine was opened in 1725 in partnership with Thomas Howard, Duke of Norfolk, and General Wade. Various minerals were mined including strontianite, hence the name of Strontian, the village built in 1724 to house the miners and their families.

The mines reached their peak in 1730, when they employed 600 men extracting silver, lead and zinc, before going gradually into decline. By then they were leased from Sir Alexander Murray by the York Building Company, an enterprise started by entrepreneurs, who built waterworks in the grounds of York House on the south side of the Strand. Using an ingenious method of pumping up water from the Thames by horsepower, they then ran it through the streets in wooden service pipes to houses in St James and Piccadilly. In 1691 the waterworks were incorporated by an act of Parliament so that, following the Jacobite Rising of 1715, when several forfeited estates were put up for sale, further legislation empowered purchasers to grant annuities on their value. Subsequently, to exploit this opportunity, Mr Case Billingsley and others bought the York Building Company.

The Company then opened a subscription at Mercer's hall for raising a joint stock and fund of £1,200,000 for purchasing forfeited and other estates in

Great Britain. The whole amount was at once eagerly subscribed and within a few months the £10 shares were worth £305. With the money the Company bought up the forfeited estates, becoming the largest landowners in Scotland. Despite financial difficulties (being almost bankrupt at one time) the Company took a lease of the lead mines at Strontian from the Duke of Norfolk and others, including Sir Alexander Murray, in 1730. Five hundred men are said to have been employed, for whom a village, known originally as New York, was built.

This meant that the population of the whole peninsula greatly increased. On Murray's own reckoning it amounted to 278 families, consisting of 408 men, 444 women and 500 children, in all adding up to 1,352 people.

Doctor Cameron encouraged the clansmen to work in the lead mines in Strontian where:

> he made it his business to oblige all concerned, and both by his advice and his example was the happy instrument of civilizing his people in those remote parts giving them a relish for trade and commerce and encouraging them to gain their bread by laudable industry and working in the mines.[28]

Obviously a physician was needed for the large workforce, not only for the men, many of whom were brought in from England, but for the wives, children and followers who came with them. This alone gives good reason why Doctor Archie established a base for his own family at Strontian. From two letters that he wrote to William MacGregor Drummond of Balhaldie, in 1732 and 1733, it appears that he was not only engaged in looking after the health of the lead miners at Strontian, but also that he acted as agent for members of his family in certain financial matters connected with these mines.[29]

In further evidence of the Camerons living in Strontian, Murray of Broughton, Prince Charles' secretary, when later hiding in Sunart, describes how Jean Cameron had fled from her home there before the Government soldiers, who had just landed, had time to set it on fire.

At the time when Murray met Jean, she had taken her children on what was then a rough track up the hill behind Strontian, to find refuge with her widowed mother.

Mrs Cameron of Dungallon lived in Glen Hurich, in Sunart, on the road which today climbs from Strontian to the pass between the mountains of Sgurr Dhomhuill and Beinn Resipol before descending by the River Dulet to the village of Polloch on Loch Sheil. Roy's Military Map of Scotland, 1747-55, shows four buildings in the glen, two near the head where the two main burns join, while that made by George Langlands, factor to the Duke of Argyll in Kintyre, in 1802, gives almost exactly similar sites of habitations. The First Statistical Account states that there were five slated houses in the area built before 1780, which suggests that that of the Camerons of Dungallon was one. Most significantly, when the Forestry Commission planted trees a little further up the glen in the last century, they pulled down the walls of a large house on the south side of the main river which the late Donald MacMillan, a descendant of people who came into Sunart after 1715, called the house of the 'Old Lairds'.

A present-day resident of Polloch, Mr J.E. Kirby, gives the following information:

> Doctor Archibald Cameron was for a time doctor to the Strontian Lead Mines on a salary of £40 per annum, treating industrial injuries and VD (allegedly introduced by English miners). He was living in Strontian at the time, in Batchelor's Hall, a 'lost' name, but almost certainly forming part of

the Old St. Mary's Scottish Episcopal Church and burial ground complex near the village centre. I think this house was later occupied by Mrs Jean Cameron of Glendessary, until she was evicted on the death of Alexander Cameron of Dungallon during the Siege of Quebec in 1757.

(see Appendix I page 211)

The main purpose of Langland's map was to show the districts then under the suzerainty of the Duke of Argyll. Sir Alexander Murray of Stanhope who bought the Ardnamurchan Peninsula, which included Sunart, at the beginning of the 18th century, nonetheless acknowledged Argyll as his overlord. From this it seems that the Camerons of Dungallon, while loyal to their chief Lochiel, must have been tenants or tacksmen of Murray in Glen Hurich.

Contemporary sources describe Archibald Cameron as doctor to the miners at Strontian, but in a letter, written in his beautiful well-formed hand, to his cousin, the red-haired Colin Campbell of Glenure, in which he apologized for failing to settle a debt, it seems to suggest that, despite his retainer from the York Building Company, Doctor Archie, paid mostly in kind by his other patients, was short of money.

Colin Campbell, son of Archie's aunt Lucy who had married Patrick Campbell of Barcaldine, had been given the estate of Glenure, at the head of Glen Creran in Appin, by his father. Later, while acting as a government factor, he would become posthumously famous as Stevenson tells how he was shot by an unknown assassin in his novel *Kidnapped.*

From his letter to Colin, it seems that Doctor Archie was attempting to make ends meet by dealing in commodities. Known to have been involved in the mining business, presumably acting as an agent for the York Building Company, he was evidently exporting locally caught herrings to Ireland. Heading his letter Strontian, 17th March 1737, he wrote:

> I have no excuse for not paying you ere now but the scarcity of money for there is no such known here, nor can I have payment of anything here but sometimes in Lead, if there was any *(way)* to advance money I would deliver the lead now, - if that fails I am afraid I can still not pay you till about a month hence when I am to have a return for some herrings I have sent to Ireland. I hope this delay won't disappoint you much, my Wife and all friends here offer their kind services to your Father and all our Cousines as does D C
>
> Your Affectionate Cousine
> Archibald Cameron[30]

Chapter 9
FAMILY LIFE

While speaking in Gaelic to his patients Doctor Archie at home spoke English, as did his brother Lochiel, and while most people in Ardnamurchan and Sunart were Presbyterians, thanks to the influence of their superior, the Duke of Argyll, the Camerons remained staunch Episcopalians.

A strange situation had developed since 1690 when, on the accession of William and Mary, the Presbyterian religion had enforced its hold. But Non-juring clergy, being Jacobites, would not take the oath of allegiance to the new monarchy. Nonetheless, despite severe restrictions against them after the Rising in 1715, while most existing clergy were pushed out of their parishes in favour of Presbyterian clergy, various compromises were made. The Second Statistical Account of Scotland, published in 1846, states that '*Protestant Episcopacy seems to have prevailed for some time before and after the revolution, a minister of that persuasion being stationed at Ardnamurchan*'.[31]

In August 1735, the Presbyterian Synod of Argyll reported that there were two Episcopalian Ministers in Lorn:

> who preached and administered the sacraments, in some places in great numbers, sometimes in privat houses, sometimes in a Tent, and for some years agoe one of them made use of a Plaid or some such thing hanged up as a screen betwixt him and the people, so as not above nine or ten appears in his view at a time, tho' numbers were within hearing.
>
> The greatest part of the gentry in Lochaber loves the Nonjuring Clergy, and their children are baptised by them, tho' they are not so madly fond of them as those in Appin.[32]

On the strength of this it seems probable that Archie's and Jean's children, like those of his brother Lochiel, were baptized in the Episcopalian faith.

It is not known how the Cameron children were educated. They may have had a private tutor, or else gone to a boarding school like their uncle Alexander or perhaps, as in their father's case, to a tutorial in Inverness. The lack of evidence regarding details of their family life can only be attributed to the focus of historians upon the approaching disruption, which would bring about such catastrophic events.

It was Alexander who, in August 1730, wrote from Boulogne to tell his brother Donald that he had decided to become a Roman Catholic. While admitting that he had *'once been a great enemie of the Roman Catholik Church'*, he added rather nervously that he wondered what *'reception it will meet with my relations'*.

Despite his fear of meeting disapproval from his family, Alexander was euphoric with happiness, believing that at last he had found a true purpose in life.

> My only greate surprise now is my former blindness in not finding the true Church, and that I should live thirtie yeares in this world without making one serious reflection, during that long space of time, upon the end and designe of my being placed on Earth.[33]

Alexander was much travelled, having been out to visit his brother Euan in Jamaica and sailed round the Caribbean. Referring to this, he told Donald:

> 'I have seen most of the splendoure and riches of this World, and have had occasion to be in some of the most beautiful Countreys but never could find out reall happiness or contentment in it: and I thank God for it, I only now can say that, I have found reall riches in possessing nothing'.

> *Finally he wrote,* 'I beg leave to offer my service to my sister *(Lochiel's wife Anne)* and to congratulate with you the good choice you have made' *before adding that he was sending* 'a case of handsome pistles' *to his brother John and* 'a pretty side pistle' *for Archie.*[34]

A few weeks after writing this he entered the philosophy course at the Scots College of Douai where he studied for two years with the Jesuits. On 30th September 1734 he entered the Society of Jesus at Tournai where, having finished his novitiate, he took simple vows after which, returning to Douai, he studied theology for four years. While there he kept in constant touch with his father, to whom his presence was an untold joy, he being his favourite son. They parted with much sadness when Alexander returned to Scotland in 1741, their sorrow only mitigated by unawareness that never would they meet again.

Chapter 10
THE CONFERENCE

In the Highlands, throughout the 1730s, speculation as to renewed rebellion to restore the exiled Stuart king ran rife amongst his supporters. A correspondence continued between King James, his son Prince Charles, and Lochiel. Rumours flew back and forth but no positive action happened until a meeting took place in Edinburgh in the spring of 1740.

Seven men sat round a table in a tavern. At the head was Donald Cameron of Lochiel. Next to him on one side sat MacLeod of MacLeod, Member of Parliament for Inverness-shire, and on the other the grotesquely portly figure of Simon Lovat, now verging on eighty years of age. All three wore the Highland dress, their plaids flung over the backs of chairs, thanks to the heat of the room.

In comparison two Lowland landowners were like pigeons compared to peacocks, only the white cravats enlivening the drabness of their clothes. One was Murray of Broughton, a slim, fair-haired Border laird, who in France had met Prince Charles. The other, his nearby neighbour Charles Stewart, Earl of Traquair. Close to them was the Duke of Perth, together with his brother Lord John Drummond.

Further down the table sat Alasdair Ruadh MacDonell, Younger of Glengarry, an officer in the Royal Scots Regiment, now in the service of King Louis XV of France. Red-haired, as his name implied, he was noticeable both for his height and as an outstandingly handsome young man.

Once more in his native country Alasdair, having abandoned his uniform for safety, was wearing the Highland garb, but in his case it was a new innovation, the *feile beag* (little wrap) or kilt.

This was a garment made of one width of material sewn into pleats, supposed to have been introduced by the manager of an iron-smelting works in Glengarry, because the belted plaid worn by his workmen was so unwieldy. A regimental tailor had suggested dividing the upper and lower parts of the plaid into separate garments and Alasdair's father, much taken with it, had ordered a set for himself. There is pictorial proof, however, that the heraldic bearers of the arms of MacFarlane of that Ilk predate this story, as they are depicted wearing the *feile beag.*

The first mention of the man, later to prove Doctor Archie's nemesis, seems to be also the only instance of any form of compatibility between Alasdair Ruadh MacDonell and his father.

Old Glengarry, a tyrant who had banished his first wife, Alasdair's mother, to a remote Hebridean island where she died, reputedly of starvation, had little or no sympathy with their son. Alasdair was brought up, largely neglected, '*in a miserable hut of turf*', Glengarry Castle having been burnt down by Government soldiers after the rising of 1715.[35] A wild boy, resentful of any form of discipline, he had been packed off to the Scots College in Paris, it would seem as a last resort. Once there, however, he had soon got into trouble, the principal, George Innes, writing in a report:

> As Glengarry has no governor tho his exercises take him out frequently and by the by may fall into bad compy for aught we can hinder especially he having no principles of religion to be a bar upon him: therefore if any accident should befall him abroad, we can't answer for it tho I'm sure we have our own fears constantly about him. His having no genius for letters, but only for fencing, dancing, rideing etc, nothing can be harder than to apply him to reading and studying the Scots law.[36]

Exasperated by Glengarry's continual bad behaviour, George Innes had finally put him and John

Gordon Dorlaithers, evidently his partner in crime, in a house by themselves, on the grounds that their frequent absences from the College and refusal to wear the College garb were having a bad effect on the discipline of the other students. This form of punishment, however, had no good effect, rather it would seem the opposite for, on 5th April 1743 Innes, writing to Bishop Smith, told him that he would never try it again. *'All the reasons one can give for their dispensation are of little avail and I have promised faithfully the like shall never happen for the future'.*[37]

Despite his bad behaviour Alasdair, on leaving the Scots College, had been gazetted as a captain in the Royal Scots Regiment serving under the King of France. As such, in 1744, he had been with the Earl Marischal at Dunkirk, waiting to start from Gravelines with what proved to be the futile naval expedition against England.

Following the ensuing debacle, MacGregor Drummond of Balhaldie, one of the exiled King James's agents in France, found a use for Young Glengarry by sending him over to Scotland to Lochiel. Specifically he went with instructions to inform Balhaldie's cousin, the Cameron chief, against trusting Murray of Broughton, James's main representative in Scotland. Lochiel, having brought the two together, informed Murray that Glengarry had told him that Balhaldie was now accusing him of telling Prince Charles to come to Scotland, with or without French assistance, to *'seat himself on the throne and leave the King at Rome'*. Murray told Glengarry that this was nonsense, thus winning him to his side.

Lochiel was fully aware that William MacGregor Drummond of Balhaldie had sent young Glengarry to him with the purpose of turning him against Murray of Broughton. Knowing Balhaldie to be a man lacking all common sense, he was hardly surprised when Glengarry produced a letter from Aeneas MacDonald, one of the seven sons of MacDonald of Kinlochmoidart who was working as a banker in Paris, calling Balhaldie a reckless provocateur.

Satisfied, on this account, that Murray, by insisting on French assistance was talking sense, Lochiel, from the head of the table, addressed the bearer of the letter:

'You will take letters to the Highlands, and the Isles, to Sir Alexander MacDonald of Sleat in Skye and other gentlemen, to ascertain the number of men they can raise. Also you must enquire into the ships and armaments, that, in the event of a Rising, they may need'. 'That I will indeed Sir.' The young man was already on his feet, as those around the table nodded their approval to the mission he was ordered to perform.

The six Highland chiefs who, together with Young Glengarry, formed that meeting in Edinburgh, signed articles of association for the restoration of the Stuart king. They promised to rise in arms, but only on the proviso that help should come from France.

A letter amongst the Stuart Papers held in the archives of Windsor Castle, from Lochiel to the exiled King James, is signed with the pseudonym 'Dan'. Dating it 22nd February 1745, he tells the king that *'the season is now far advancing'*, and that, as yet,*' they had no return from their friends in England'*.

On 11th May 1745 the victory at Fontenoy of Marshal Saxe, in command of the Irish Brigade of the French army, over the combined British, Dutch, Hanoverian and Austrian forces led by the Duke of Cumberland, caused fevered excitement amongst the Jacobites in France. For Prince Charles it seemed that this was the moment, a heaven sent chance to carry out the invasion of the Highlands of Scotland for which, waiting in Paris, he had grown so impatient to begin. Surely King Louis would now agree to help him! He must realize that the present situation offered a unique chance to draw the British army from Flanders should a

Jacobite rebellion in Scotland take place.

It was towards the end of June 1745, when King Louis received a letter from Prince Charles:

> Monsieur Mon Oncle, Having in vain sought to gain access to Your Majesty in the hope of obtaining from your generosity the help I need to play a part worthy of my birth. I have decided to make myself known for my own deeds and to undertake alone a course of action the success of which could be guaranteed by quite a small measure of assistance. I flatter myself that Your Majesty will not refuse me this.[38]

Louis discussed the possibilities with his ministers while beyond the windows of the Palace of Versailles fountains cascaded in brilliance beneath the heat of the mid-summer sun. Scotland, the old ally of France, had been encouraged to fight the English across the Border to distract English forces from France for centuries past. The results had not always been successful. A French force sent to Scotland as Henry VIII invaded France had proved very expensive without bringing great results. Under the King's direction the ministers agreed to prevaricate, unwilling to commit themselves to an undertaking which might involve not only too much expense, but also a great loss of life.

From Scotland Alasdair Ruadh travelled to tell Prince Charles specifically not to attempt an invasion without the support of a French army. On landing he hastened to Paris but was told there by acquaintances that he had come too late. Alasdair, on hearing this, looked to find employment. If he could not prevent the Prince from making this rash attempt at invasion, he must somehow find some other means of turning the situation to his own advantage.

Chapter 11
THE SUMMONS

Far away from Paris, on the northwest coast of Scotland, excitement amongst the Jacobites increased to fever pitch as rumours passed from mouth to mouth that Prince Charles would soon arrive. Spring was turning to summer, the cattle were being put to the hills when, on 15th May, word reached Blair Castle that he was actually on his way.

From Drummond Castle the Duke of Perth, the leading Jacobite in Scotland, not yet deprived of his title by the Hanoverian government, sent a messenger with a letter to warn Lochiel. Horrified and confused as to what was intended Lochiel made the dispatch rider stay the night before sending him back with his reply:

> I had the honour of your letter last night and carefully perused the papers you sent inclosed, the contents whereof give me the outmost concern. I find everything so strangely concerted, I am sorry to say, in such a confused and undigested manner, that I don't know what judgement to form of it, and what measures to take. The principall person *(the Prince)* is not to be blamed, but whoever advised him to undertake it (without anyone thing that I can see prepared for that purpose) has a great deal to answer for; I am at a loss how to act.
> Besydes the Countrey, especially the Isles are destitute of all sorts of provisions and some of the poor people have actually died already for want of food. Every thing considered, I fear the Consequence, but I pray God it may turn out contrary to the present idea I have of it.[39]

Shortly afterwards, Murray of Broughton, who was to become Prince Charles's secretary, set out to give warning of what was about to happen to the Highland chiefs. In his Memoirs he describes how *'I went under a borrowed name, and pretended to come from England to buy wood'*. Leaving Edinburgh he went to Kippen, and from thence to Drummond Castle:

> where I staid till the evening following, and then set out for Lochaber. The second night I reached *(MacDonald of)* Keppoch's house, and after talking to him about the Prince's scheme...I set out next day for Lochyell's house at Achnacarry, but being known by all there, I stopped at an Inn about a mile from the house, and sent a Gentleman, who had gone with me as a guide, to acquaint Lochyell of my arrival.
> He soon after met me in his garden, (*Lochiel had just designed a new garden close to his great wooden house)* and told me, he had received the letter by express from the Duke of Perth, and sent it by his brother (*the Doctor*) to Lovat with whom Macleod (*Norman, 19th Chief of MacLeod, M.P. for Inverness-shire)* then was, and expected he would return the next day.[40]

Lochiel at first could not believe what Murray told him, saying that he had not looked on the letter from the Duke of Perth as important:

> not imagining the Prince was yet determined to come to Scotland, having had no prior intelligence from him for so many months, nor any accounts from Lord Traquair.[41]

While they walked together along the newly laid out paths edged with low cut box hedges dividing the plots of beds where roses would soon be in flower, he lifted his face to the sun. The idea of war seemed preposterous. The country was sublimely peaceful, warm with the promise of summer, oak trees always the last to bear leaves, now olive green with new growth. The cuckoos had come and the warblers, and the air seemed alive with their song. Measuring his steps beside that of his visitor Lochiel felt a sense of unreality as the import of what Murray was saying struck home.

He explained that the letters he had sent to the Prince through Lord Traquair, to dissuade him from making an immediate landing in Scotland, had been returned to him because Traquair, having failed to find anyone willing to carry them to France for less than an enormous sum, had simply sent them back with Macleod. Finally he had managed to send the letters to the Prince with Young Glengarry whose loyalty, although later so questionable, at that time appeared to be genuine enough.

Murray then made the point, that *'although Traquair had failed them, there was no reason to doubt the English would appear...'* and he continued:

> I then gave it freely as my opinion, that considering his Royal Highness had advertised his friends here of his design so many months before, and though they had objected to his coming without troops, yet they nevertheless engaged to join him; so taking things in that light, I did not see how they could in honour excuse themselves.
> To this he replied that he was extremely glad I was come, not having considered things in that light... He then acknowledged he did not see how any man of honour could get off, adding that although Balhaldie, acting as their agent, had presented things in the wrong light, yet it could be no reason for refusing to join the Prince, especially as he was to throw himself naked into their arms, and thereby shew the entire confidence he had in them; so, for his own part, he would not delay one moment to give him all the assistance in his power.
> Next day Doctor Cameron returned, and informed us that he had taken an opportunity to shew the letter to Lord Lovat and MacLeod together: that Lovat before he had made an end

> of reading it, said in a passion, *'that he should not be allowed to land, and that if he did, by G-d no man should join him';* that upon this, Macleod stopped him, desiring he would not be in such a hurry, saying *'he did not look upon things to be so bad, nor was he to be used in that manner, and that they ought seriously to consider of it; and that after much conversation, they proposed a letter should be written, dissuading him from landing'.*[42]

Both Murray and Lochiel were astonished by Lovat's outburst, particularly as he had been one of the main instigators of the plan to bring Prince Charles to Scotland to raise a rebellion in his father's name. Lochiel, on reflection, took this to be *'only a sudden sally, and that he would nevertheless join, when he saw his neighbours take the field...He likewise further gave it as his opinion, that his Lordship had already gone to such lengths, that, did things come to an open rupture, his appearing seemed to be the only chance he had to save himself'.*

Murray then proposed that he should go to Glenelg to meet Sir Alexander MacLeod, who was on his way to the Isle of Skye, to tell him to find reliable people on Uist to look out for the Prince's arrival. He would then go across country to meet young Clanranald. This being agreed, it was decided to send express messages to MacDonald of Keppoch, Stewart of Ardshiel, and Old Glengarry who, *'for very substantial reasons'* had not been let into the secret.

Writing that *'I set out next morning in company with Doctor Cameron, Lochiel's brother and John MacDonald, son of the Laird of Scotus, and the evening following we reach'd that Gentleman's house in Knoydart',* Murray was then warned by MacDonald's eldest son that, *'because of the risk of discovery by the Officers of the garrison at Bernera'* it was dangerous to continue to Glenelg. Accepting, therefore, John MacDonald's suggestion that he should remain in his father's house, he left it to Macleod *'to appoint some other part of the Country where we would be less liable to be observed'.*[43]

Lochiel, according to a long held tradition, was supervising the planting of a beech hedge beside the river Arkaig when a breathless runner brought the news that the Prince was at Borrodale in Arisaig. He had come in a French ship, which was lying in the inlet of the sea known as Loch nan Uamh.

Stalling for time in committing himself to what he knew could only be an exceptionally dangerous and probably futile undertaking, he sent the message on to his brother Archie, telling him to go in his place.

Chapter 12
HIS BROTHER'S MAN

It is not known whether Archie was in Glenkingie, it being harvest time, or at Strontian, when the message from his brother, probably carried by a runner from Achnacarry, reached him. Both places are, in fact, much the same distance from Loch nan Uamh.

If Archie was in Sunart, as seems likely in view of his employment there, it would have been but a short journey by boat across Loch Sheil to the south-west shore of Moidart. From there he would have taken the track, hard packed by the hooves of cattle driven down from Skye and the north west mainland to the cattle markets further south. Walking with the long strides of a man of the hills, he would have swung along the twelve miles or so in little more than two hours.

It was late July, bees hummed in the heather, the scent strong in the air. The sun was near its zenith, the earth itself now warm, yet Archie barely noticed it so deeply troubled was his mind. When he was only a boy of eight he had seen his father exiled, driven from his home and his country, and aware of his mother's misery, he had known what it was to be frightened in case the red-coated soldiers came. He had joined in his brother's struggle to provide for the family and their clan. Only now, after nearly thirty years, had some sort of stability been achieved. Another war would bring ruination, setting it all back to what it had been before. He could not believe there was any sense in it. Much the best, in fact the only sensible thing, would be for the French ship to raise anchor and head back the way she had come.

But he had to carry out his instructions. Donald, in his message, had been specific as to what they were. Acting in his name, he was not to commit them to anything. He must assure the Prince of their loyalty, but be vague about how they would act.

Reaching the south side of Loch nan Uamh, he was rowed across to the *du Teillay*, lying at anchor in the Sound.

Prince Charles was aboard where Archie found him. It is not known if by then the Prince had abandoned the black garb of the clerical scholar of the Scots College in which he had sailed from France, or was wearing the Highland dress of trews with a plaid and the blue velvet bonnet in which he is so frequently described.

Archie, when in France, had heard that King James was a man with a melancholy countenance, apparently very withdrawn. Expecting something similar in the person of his son, he was amazed, as he reached the deck of the *du Teillay,* to be greeted by a young man, obviously strong and agile although he was of slender build who, speaking with a French accent, raised him to his feet as he knelt before him, greeting him warmly as a friend. Charmed immediately, Archie nonetheless spoke with reservation, obeying his brother's instructions, despite his spontaneous liking for this altogether surprising individual.

All that is known about their meeting comes from the pen of Sir John MacDonald, one of the 'Seven Men of Moidart' who had sailed with the Prince from France.

Following his brother's instructions, Archie *'talked lightly a great deal but promised nothing'.* But he then added significantly, as events would later prove, *'that if he joined the Prince's standard he would be amongst the last to quit it'.*[44]

Charles, dissatisfied, and aware that Archie was prevaricating, sent another messenger to Lochiel, ordering him to come to meet him in person, which Lochiel, for whom Charles's father was sovereign, felt himself bound to obey.

Wasting no time he left Achnacarry to arrive at his brother John's house at Fassifern (the property he had sold to him some years before) in the early hours of the morning. Dragged from his bed, John was extremely surprised to see him, asking why he came at such an hour. On Lochiel explaining his mission John, the successful business man and burgess of Glasgow, knew at once that his brother, in what seemed to him mistaken loyalty, was heading for inevitable disaster. *'What troops had the Prince brought with him? What money? What arms?'* were the first questions he asked. Lochiel replied, with all honesty, that he believed he had brought nothing other than himself and a few companions, but he then assured his brother that he was going to have nothing to do with the affair and would do his utmost to prevent Charles from making such a rash attempt.

John foresaw the result, word of the Prince's charismatic charm having been noised about.

'Brother,' he said, *'I know you better than you know yourself. If this Prince once sets his eyes on you, he will make you do whatever he pleases'.* He begged him to go no further on his way to Borrodale but to come into the house and write a letter, explaining his views to Charles. *'No'* came the answer, *'I need at least to wait upon him and give my reasons in person for declining to join him, which admit of no reply'.* John could argue no further. With a growing premonition of tragedy, he could only watch his brother ride away.

As it turned out the Prince was back on board ship by the 30th July, that being the day when the log of the *du Teillay* recorded that *'un grand chaloupe,'* a large oared boat, came alongside with some *seigneurs*, one of whom was Lochiel.

John's words of warning proved useless for Charles, having listened to Lochiel's protestations that it was mad to proceed with a Rising until at least an army came from France, merely told him that in a few days he would erect the royal standard and proclaim to the people of Britain that Charles Stuart is come over to claim the crown of his ancestors, to win it, or perish in the attempt and *'Lochiel, who, my father has often told me was our firmest friend, may stay at home, and learn from the newspapers the fate of his prince'.*

'No', replied Lochiel, *'I shall share the fate of my prince, and so shall every man over whom nature or fortune hath given me any power'.*[45]

The die was cast. He had given his word. Now there could be no return.

Lochiel still had his brother Archie to deal with. Archie who swore he would never take arms and fight. So great was their disagreement that:

> when he had mustered his Clan, and set up his Standard, he found that his brother had left him in disgust. This gave him a good deal of Disquietude, for he could not bear the thought that one so nearly related to him, should have a separate Interest. Upon which he sent a Messenger to him with an Order, requiring immediate Attendance. The Doctor obeyed, but could not so easily be wrought upon to concur with his Brother's new Schemes.He remonstrated, in the strongest terms, upon the unsurmountable Obstacles that he foresaw would attend the Undertaking, and the terrible consequences of a Miscarriage, Lochiel, however, would take no Denial, telling him, that he did not want the assistance of his Sword or his Valour, but only desired he would attend him as his Companion, that he might always have the Advantage of his Advice and Skill, in case the fortune of War should render them necessary. The Doctor, how ill soever he thought of the cause, yet his affection for his Brother, and the many signal Obligations he lay under to him, at length prevailed over other Considerations, and he submitted to share his Brother's fate whatever it should be'.[46]

It is claimed that it was Lochiel's wife Anne who finally persuaded Archie to join her husband, pointing out that '*he loved his brother Lochiel, who was his only support, and forced him out under pain of his highest displeasure; even threatening to pistol him if he did not comply; and insisted that it was the least thing he could do to attend his person, and cure him of any hurt he might receive*'.[47]

Chapter 13
PREPARATIONS FOR WAR

His mind once made up to follow his brother Doctor Archie wasted no time in forcing his wife's people to join him. There is a statement from John Cameron, (The Presbyterian minister who followed Prince Charles' army throughout the campaign), when a prisoner, in which he declares that Doctor Cameron came to his brother-in-law, Alexander Cameron of Dungallon:

> and forcibly brought from thence five hundred men, mostly of the name of Cameron, threatening them that if they did not come off directly *'he would burn their houses and cut them in pieces'* while another member of the same clan stated that *'Doctor Cameron killed four of his cows before he consented to go with him'*.[48]

This sounds so out of character with what we know of Doctor Archie that it is hard to believe. One wonders if perhaps John Cameron, as a prisoner, invented it as an excuse to prove his own innocence in rising to fight against King George. If he was speaking the truth, or at least part of it, the reluctance of men to go and fight at harvest time may have resulted in Archie being forced to use desperate methods to make them obey his brother's call to arms. Prince Charles probably failed to realize that his landing in Scotland could not have been worse timed for people whose lives and those of their families depended entirely on what they could raise from the land. The four cows may have been killed to feed the men coming in from the glens to enlist under the Prince's banner, but for evidence of this being done under Doctor Archie's orders there is only the word of the chaplain who, under interrogation, was probably a very frightened man.

Once resigned to involvement in the forthcoming rebellion, Doctor Archie began preparations for the part he would have to play. While his wife Jean, who seems to have been the dominant force in the marriage, organized some of the women to cut strips of linen and roll them for bandages, others, together with children, went out to gather the sphagnum moss that was so effective for healing wounds. Packed into saddle-bags it would remain damp enough for a period of several months.

Meanwhile men were despatched to find straight pieces of wood which, split lengthways with an axe, could be used as splints to keep broken bones in place.

Archie himself gathered together the saws that he would need for amputations, and thread made of fine horsehair for stitching wounds. He had few anaesthetics apart from a small amount of laudanum (opium dissolved in spirits of wine) the panacea of the day, and a quantity of wine and brandy to ease both shock and pain.

His equipment organized, he was ready to lead the men of Dungallon north up the shore of Loch Linnhe and from thence, following the River Lochy, to the rendezvous at Achnacarry, a distance of some thirty miles.

To his amazement, on arriving at his brother's house, he found him holding as prisoner none other than Captain John Scott, the officer in charge of a detachment of Royal Scots sent to reinforce the garrison of Fort William. Captain Scott left a lively account of his adventure. About to cross the River Spean at High Bridge he heard the sound of bagpipes and *'saw some Highlanders on the other side of the bridge skipping and leaping about with swords and firelocks in their hands'.* He accordingly sent a sergeant and his own servant to find out what was happening, whereupon, in a skirmish, a sergeant and three other soldiers were killed and sixty men, including several officers, taken prisoner.

The captured man, taken to Achnacarry, was *'treated more like a friend and a brother than an enemy and a prisoner. Captain Scott's wounded arm was cared for by Anne Cameron, Lochiel's wife herself'.*

On a message being sent to the garrison at Fort William the Governor, the elderly Archibald Campbell, refused to send a surgeon to Achnacarry, whereupon Lochiel despatched Scott to Fort William under parole. His horse, a striking grey thoroughbred called Tiendrish, however, was kept later to be given to Prince Charles.

In the fields beside the Water of Arkaig hay was being scythed, but the fields adjacent to the great wooden house resembled nothing so much as a fairground as men, led by Lochiel's tacksmen, came in, some armed with pikes, swords and axes, others carrying targes. These were made of thick leather which, while not entirely proof against bullets, could withstand the point of a sword. Although tartans in those days were not as we understand them now, they wore the great plaid, the *feile mor*, a useful garment which could be used to cover the body completely when sleeping on open ground. This would have been made from material coloured by the natural dyes of local plants, and they would have worn in their bonnets the clan badges of oak or crowberry.

Even on a still day the noise was deafening. The shouting and cursing in Gaelic, the stamping of hooves and neighing of horses echoing through the glen on the warm air. One holdup followed another, as horses cast shoes which had to be replaced, and some of the men coming in from the hills appeared late. But at last all the weapons were distributed and everything was ready. Formed into lines they were to be followed by the baggage train of ponies, pulling carts and sledges, or slipes as in Scotland they are called, holding both quantities of oatmeal, the staple diet of Highland men, and also Doctor Archie's medical supplies. With them came the women, the camp followers who in those days trailed behind every army, working largely as cooks.

Clansmen came from Locharkaig and Glendessary over the pass into the north end of Glenfinnan; others from Sunart would have come up Lochsheil, while Camerons from Locheilside probably came roughly by the route of the present main road, but avoiding Corpach, for the Hanoverian garrison was there.

But tradition has it that the main body of the Camerons came over the hills from Achnacarry and down to where the viaduct now stands, surely with banners flying and pipers playing.

On 19th August 1745, it was late in the afternoon when Prince Charles and those with him clustered around the royal banner, proud symbol fluttering in a light breeze. All had eyes on the hill, one question and one only in their minds. Would he come with his Camerons or would Lochiel go back on his word?

Several began murmuring, whispering amongst themselves that the whole had been nothing but a ruse. But then they heard the sound of the bagpipes, so faint at first that it could have been the mewing of gulls or of buzzards circling overhead, then stronger until the strains of the familiar Cameron tune, the *Piobaireachd Dhomnuill Duibh,* became unmistakable, a sound so thrilling that even the strongest of doubters felt their breath catch in their throats.

Reaching the watershed, Donald of Lochiel and his brother, marching at the head of their men, were the first to catch a glimpse of the near shore of Loch Sheil. There, below, at the head of the loch, on a stretch of green land, a concourse of men surrounded the standard, a handsome banner of red and white silk which they knew to be the Princes' own, and at sight of it the clansmen cheered, dragging off their bonnets and throwing them into the air.

Heads raised below watched as these sturdy men, sure-footed as the deer, their tartans blending with the heather in bloom, came down the steep hillside towards Loch Sheil, a sight none of those would ever forget.

'Never have I seen anything so quaintly pleasing as the march of the troop of Highlanders as they descended a steep mountain by a zig zag path' wrote Sir John MacDonald, one of those standing beside the Prince on the meadowland near where the River Finnan runs into the head of Loch Sheil.

Note. It is most probable that the Prince's banner at this early stage did not have the words 'Tandem Triumphans' embroidered upon the red square in the centre, but by the time the army reached Perth the 'Scots Magazine' of September 1745 recorded the words. It is thought that there was more than one banner, as sometimes it was described as having a narrow blue edge.

Chapter 14
THE RUTHVEN BARRACKS

'All was confused' wrote Colonel O'Sullivan, remembering the start of the march. He continued to describe how the Clan Cameron, led by Lochiel, was divided into sections commanded by two lieutenant-colonels. One was his brother Doctor Archie who, if O'Sullivan is correct, must have abandoned the provision made to Donald that he would follow him only as a doctor, never as a soldier bearing arms. The other was his uncle Ludovic Cameron of Torcastle, son of old Sir Ewen's marriage to his third wife. Behind them came Archie's brother-in-law, Major Alexander Cameron of Dungallon, described as *'a charming young man',* whom the Prince made his standard-bearer on the march.

Archie's elder brother Alexander, returned from France as a Roman Catholic priest, like the Presbyterian John Cameron, was to minister to the clan throughout the campaign. There was also an Episcopalian clergyman, the Camerons being the only clan to have three clerics throughout the Rising.

On 22nd August Prince Charles moved to Kinlocheil. On the next day he lodged at John Cameron's house of Fassifern before marching on to Moy. It was here that he plucked a white rose from the garden which was to become the Jacobite emblem. Two days later he set out again for Invergarry, stronghold of MacDonell of Glengarry. This was the man whom Lochiel's and Archie's other uncle Allan (son of their grandfather's second marriage) had specifically mentioned in his letter of advice to Lochiel, as one to try to placate. It is probable that Allan was referring to some argument over land.

Of Glengarry's sons Alasdair Ruadh, (he who had attended the meeting in Edinburgh) the second eldest and much like him in character, had been taken prisoner while sailing from France to fight for Prince Charles and was now in the Tower of London. It was Aeneas, his eldest son, by all accounts a nicer man who, in view of his father's age, was now to lead his clan into battle.

At Invergarry the Prince was joined, not only by a large contingent of MacDonells under Aeneas' command, but by 260 Appin Stewarts, led not by their chief but by Charles Stewart of Ardshiel, a giant of a man on an equally enormous white horse, which he called the Muilleach, having bought him from a miller in Leith.

That night the Jacobite army seized the Corrieyairack Pass, thus gaining direct access into Badenoch, from where lay a direct route to Blair Atholl and the south.

It was from the foot of the Corrieyairack Pass, before the army reached Dalwhinnie that, against Prince Charles' better judgement, the chiefs decided amongst themselves that the newly built barracks at Ruthven, near Kingussie, must be taken:

> not only to have the country free, but on account of the quantity of oatmeal yt might be found there, it was proposed to attempt it by stratagem the night following, but the Chevalier upon enquirey, finding it was flanked, and he having no cannon nor conveniency for making of scaling ladders, judged it more proper to let it alone as a place of no consequence and unequall to the lives of those who might fall at the attempt.[49]

The chiefs, however, insisted that an attack on the barracks should be made. Consequently next day, 29th August, Colonel O'Sullivan, the portly Irish soldier of fortune who had sailed with the Prince from France, and Doctor Archie, with between sixty and a hundred

Camerons according to different reports, set off to reach Ruthven sometime after it was dark.

The barracks, built in two blocks as recently as 1719 following the Rising of 1715, stood on the site of a castle which had belonged to Alexander Stewart, the famous Wolf of Badenoch, terror of the district for miles around. Doctor Archie and O'Sullivan with their band of men took the stables, just a few yards from the barracks, without difficulty. Very early the next morning the two of them, together with one Gordon, who pretended to be well acquainted with the place, made a parcel of what is described as *'some combustible stuff to be set on fire at the back door or sally port'*. But as there were two steps up to the door it made it very difficult to put the inflammatory device in place. Meanwhile shots rained down on them, fired by muskets through the gun loops in the walls. Confused by the intensity of the fire, they were not to know that the barracks, built for 120 soldiers, held only twelve men. Archie himself, if Henderson is to be believed, as part of the agreement with his brother, did not carry a weapon, but his men returned the fire with the arquebuses with which some of them were armed.

The shots rattling against the new, strongly built walls blasted off a few chips of granite. One man was killed and three badly wounded as they tried to blow in the door. Only one of the garrison, foolish enough to try to see what was happening, had his head shot off as he peered above the wall.

The portly O'Sullivan is said to have hidden in a barn while all this was going on, until it became plain, that with only swords and a few, mostly antiquated guns, the attackers could not force the barrack defences. Doctor Archie's part in the action is not mentioned, but it may have been he who ordered the somewhat ignominious withdrawal,[50] the Prince himself then reminding the chiefs, rather acidly, that he had vetoed the attack in the first place.

The details of the march that followed, through Atholl and down to Perth are too well known to need repetition. Unforgettable moments included the entrance into Perth, as Charles rode into the city on the grey horse called Tiendrish. The evening sunlight slanting low in the sky, dazzled the eyes of spectators, who gasped with delight at sight of the gold braid on the waistcoat of the tartan suit, and the white cockade on the blue velvet bonnet as, with the grey horse's reins in one hand, the Prince sat so easily astride.

Chapter 15
THE NETHERBOW PORT

Then it was on to Edinburgh where the army camped at Gray's Mill, near Slateford, two miles to the south-west of the city. From there Prince Charles sent a summons to the magistrates, ordering them:

> to receive us, as you are in duty bound to do...We promise to preserve all the rights and liberties of the city, and the particular property of every one of his Majesty's subjects. But if any opposition be made to us we cannot answer for the consequences, being firmly resolved at any rate to enter the city, and in that case, if any of the inhabitants are found in arms against us, they must not expect to be treated as prisoners of war.
>
> (Signed) CHARLES, PRINCE REGENT
>
> *From our camp, 16th September 1745.*[51]

Greatly alarmed, Provost Stewart and the city magistrates sent a deputation to the Prince asking for the details of his terms. Received by Murray of Broughton they were told that they must open the gates of the city to the Jacobite army and surrender all the arms and ammunition they possessed. Asking for time to consider, they were told they could only have three hours. Emboldened by the news that Sir John Cope's army, which had sailed from Inverness, was now in the Firth of Forth, the dignitaries then sent another deputation asking for more time but Charles, through Murray, told them *'to get them gone'*.

He then ordered Lochiel *'to putt his people under arms to be ready to march upon a minute's warning'*. With Murray, who was very familiar with the district, acting as their guide, the detachment passed within earshot of the Castle, so close that they could actually hear the soldiers of the garrison calling their rounds in the faint light of early dawn. Totally undetected they reached the Netherbow Port in the city wall at what is now the end of the High Street above the Canongate.

When Lochiel demanded admission from the porter this was, as expected, curtly refused.

It then being daylight, Murray suggested they should retire to what was at that time called St Leonard's Hills (now Arthur's Seat). Going to the rear of the detachment he began to lead the way, but hardly had he done so before the rumble of a coach, coming down the High Street towards the Netherbow gate, was heard.

It was, in fact, the very coach which, having brought the deputies to meet Murray for their second and, as it had proved, unsuccessful meeting, had returned them to their city homes. Empty, it was now trundling back over the cobbles, heading for the stables in the Canongate, beyond the city wall. As the porter, amazingly unsuspecting, possibly half asleep, pulled open the heavy gates, Lochiel recognized his opportunity and shouted an order in Gaelic to advance.

Dashing through the gate his sword drawn, his brother Archie among the Cameron men behind him, he led the charge. The terrified porter reeled back before the horde of bearded savages, armed with pikes and swords and yelling at the tops of their voices as they surged past him, before he could even think of trying to push the heavy gates together.

Edinburgh was taken. Only the castle, its canons trained on the city, remained defiant of assault. The people were surprised when they woke to find the town occupied by the rebel army with none of the expected violence or pillaging that had filled them with such dread.

At a little before noon Lochiel's regiment, seven hundred strong, marched three in line, with their pipers playing and banners flying, to surround the Mercat Cross in the middle of the city's High Street. Arriving they made a wide circle from the end of the

Luckenbooth to below the Cross. The bells of the High Kirk rang out until, in a sudden silence, Ross Herald proclaimed the manifesto *'in the name of King James the eighth of Great Britain'*. Ladies at the window waved their handkerchiefs. The crowds in the street cheered.

Later that same day, as the Prince and his entourage arrived at Holyrood Palace, most of the townspeople turned out to view the spectacle in the surrounding Park.

CHAPTER 16
PRESTONPANS

Unused as he was to court protocol, Doctor Archie may have even been relieved when news reached Holyrood Palace that General Cope had disembarked his troops at Dunbar. *'Has he, by God!'* exclaimed Prince Charles. So the Jacobite army, encamped in the King's park, moved on to Duddingston, where Murray reported that:

> The chevalier putt himself att the head of his small army, *(where)* drawing his sword, he said *'gentlemen I have thrown away the scabbard, with God's assistance I don't doubt of making you a free and happy people, Mr Cope shall not escape us as he did in the Highlands.*[52]

The army was still at Duddingston when an argument broke out amongst the chiefs of the clans as to their position in the line of battle. Charles himself suggested then that lots should be drawn, and upon this being decided, the combined force of Macdonalds drew the left, while the Camerons and Stewarts of Appin drew the lot for the right. This being hotly resented by the Macdonalds, who claimed that King Robert the Bruce, after Bannockburn, had awarded them the place of honour on the right, Lochiel sensibly suggested that he would willingly let the MacDonalds march from the left the next morning to wheel round to form the right of the army as a whole.

On the afternoon of 20th September the Jacobite army bypassed the village of Tranent to take up a new position south of a stretch of bog on the other side of which, in a stubble field close to the North Sea, Cope's army was arrayed. In the evening, just as it was getting dark, the local landlord, Robert Anderson, came to Prince Charles and told him that, when out shooting, he had found a safe way across the bog. During the night the Highland army crossed this in single file until, on reaching the hard ground by the coast they once again formed rank. General Cope, in the first light, thinking he saw a line of bushes, was surprised as the sun rose higher to see them become fighting men. Desperately he tried to array his army even as the Highlanders, under Lord George Murray, were upon him, swords making deadly carnage as they charged.

As trained, they struck the horses on the nose, so that the terrified animals swung round to bolt into the cavalry lines behind them causing mayhem as they went. The result was a total riot, gloriously remembered by the Jacobites for evermore.

At least three hundred and fifty men in Cope's army were either wounded or killed while, as estimated by Murray *'not above three or four officers were killed, and seventy or eighty officers and soldiers wounded on the Jacobite side'*. They included James Mor MacGregor, Rob Roy's eldest son who, when felled by five bullets, famously shouted to his clansmen, *'I am not dead, and by God, I shall see if any of you does not do his duty'.* Murray reckoned that, in the government army, about four times above the official number had been either killed or wounded.

Alexander Carlyle, son of the minister of the Kirk of Prestonpans, was an eyewitness of the carnage on the battlefield. Greatly daring he managed to retrieve the medicine chest of Cope's army. Lord Elcho rode past like a madman shouting to all within hearing to ask where a publick house could be found, ale being better than nothing to relieve the agony of wounds. Carlyle then met Lochiel. *'who was polish'd and gentle and who ordered a soldier to make all the enquiry he could about the medicine chests'*.[53]

Doctor Archie is mentioned, in nearly every history of the time, for the attention that he gave to the wounded following the battle of Prestonpans. Prince

Charles had ordered humane treatment of the enemy and Doctor Archie is known to have stayed up, without rest, for forty-eight hours tending the wounds of fallen men – so many suffering from the slashes of sharp-edged deadly swords.

Henderson describes a dramatic incident when:

> One Cameron of Kinloch, a man scarce five feet two inches high, very meagre and thin to look upon, was yet so strong as to be able to grapple with any in the whole army, and so skilful at the broad-sword that he had few equals…came up to an officer in the King's army who was at the head of his company, made his honours very handsomely with his sword, and desired him to yield himself prisoner. The captain looked on him with disdain, and condemning his mean appearance, thrust at him with his small sword which he had in his hand. Cameron parried him, and then struck him so dexterously upon the wrist, that he cut off his hand, which, with the sword, fell to the ground. The officer directly yielded, and Cameron scraped together some crumbled earth off the field, which he put in his handkerchief, applied it to the gentleman's stump, stopped the bleeding, and then introduced him to Doctor Cameron, who in the most tender and sympathizing manner, dressed his wound, as he did those of several other prisoners, and when it was proposed to put all to the sword, Lochiel so far rejected the overture, that he declared, if any such thing happened, he would abandon the cause.[54]

Archie, exhausted after two full days without sleep, was at least spared the trauma of seeing a family member killed. Not so fortunate was the young Stuart Threipland, son of a Perthshire laird, the only one, other than Cameron, of the twenty-five doctors specifically named as having taken part in the campaign. Threipland's elder brother David, conspicuous riding a thoroughbred black charger, was killed by a shot from a musket as he galloped after fleeing dragoons. Stuart, later to become a close friend of Archie's, was amongst the men who buried him below an ash tree, near the field where he fell. His death was just one of the tragedies that cast a shadow over the euphoria of Prince Charles' triumph on that never to be forgotten day.

Chapter 17
'HEAVEN'S DARLING'

Returning to Edinburgh, Prince Charles made Lochiel Governor of the city and it is a reasonable assumption too, that by now he had appointed Archie one of his *aide-de-camps*. The rumour then circulated that he would make an assault on the Castle with a force of his men. Nothing of the sort happened, although as attempts were made to prevent supplies reaching the fortress the Governor of the Castle, the octogenarian General Preston, ordered a cannonade. Several houses were demolished and Lochiel, making an inspection, was hit on the shoulder by flying stones. He was not badly hurt, however, and his brother, no doubt admonishing him for foolhardiness, applied salve to the bruised skin.

Six days later the siege was called off. The cast iron cannons cooled into silence, no longer deafening the ears of the citizens, who returned to near normal life.

All attention then was fixed on Holyrood Palace where the Prince won the hearts, not only of the women who literally fell at his feet, but also of most of the men. Doctor Archie is not named specifically as taking part in the festivities. A family man, used to plain living, who appears to have been rather shy, he may have been overwhelmed, perhaps to the point of disapproval, of the adulation heaped upon Charles.

Typical of the near hysterical adoration that the Prince's very presence inspired, is a letter from Miss Christian Threipland, a Perthshire lady, to a friend:

> ......Oh had you beheld my beloved Hero, you must confess he is a gift from Heaven; but then, besides his outward appearance, which is absolutely the best figure I ever saw, such Vivacity, such piercing Wit, woven with a clear Judgement and an active Genius, and allowed by all to have a Capacity apt to receive such impressions as are not usually stampt on every brain: in short Madam, he is the Top of Perfection and Heaven's Darling.[55]

Chapter 18
'MORE LIKE CHIMNEY SWEEPS THAN SOLDIERS'

The Highland army left Edinburgh to begin the march to England at the beginning of November. Henderson describes how:

> Lochiel was the last to leave the city, and coming to Lauder, he was informed that indiscretions had been committed by some of his private men, and being told who they were, he went with his whip in among them and lashed them severely on account of their misbehaviour.[56]

This does not sound typical of the man who, on Henderson's evidence, had so recently, on the battlefield of Prestonpans, sworn to abandon the Prince's cause if any of the enemy prisoners were slaughtered. Nonetheless the Highlanders, particularly when drunk, were known to run amok and Lochiel, wielding his whip, had to enforce discipline to keep control.

By then, as the army headed for Carlisle, the weather became increasingly atrocious. Archie Cameron and his fellow doctors were largely occupied in caring for men who, accustomed to walking over grass and heather, now found their feet bruised and blistered by the stones of the rough road, their shoes, made of hide and tied with thongs, being totally worn out or else largely in holes. Used as they were to long marches all were feeling the strain, and many were suffering from colds and influenza due to the appalling weather. Prince Charles himself, who insisted on walking at the head of his soldiers, was soon so physically exhausted that he had to lean on the shoulders of two of them for support. The euphoria of those autumn days had gone. Now it was a question of endurance in cold and clinging mud.

Nearly five weeks later, on 4 December, when the vanguard entered Derby, they were:

> a crew of shabby, lousy, pitiful look'd fellows; mixed up with old men and boys; dressed in dirty plaids, and as dirty shoes, without breeches; and wore their stockings made of plaid, not much above halfway up their legs, some without shoes, or next to none, and with their plaids thrown over their shoulders. Had they been unarmed they would have appeared more like a parcel of chimney sweeps than soldiers.[57]

Plainly, from this description, the army surgeons were fully occupied with many forms of illness. However, during the march into England, Archie's name is not mentioned, appearing only in the records when the army was making its return.

Famously, it was with the greatest reluctance that Prince Charles, on the advice of the commanders of his army, agreed to retreat north from Derby.

The Jacobites had reached Kendal when, on 15th December, some people at a market began to mob a party of Hussars which was marching with the Duke of Perth, a nobleman universally loved by the men. The country people, their courage no doubt amplified by ale, set about them in fear, rather than anger, believing themselves about to be robbed of all their animals and possessions by these savage looking men with their long hair and beards, in strange clothes by this time hardly distinguishable with wear. As the main body came up and was informed of it, they breathed nothing but revenge, threatening to burn the town about their ears, unless ransomed by the sum of twenty thousand pounds.

The magistrates were dumbfounded, being quite unable to produce such a sum. One of them at last, facing up to Doctor Archie, told him that none of the townspeople was involved. That it had all happened on a market day wherein offenders could easily be distinguished. The Doctor, seeing the point of his argument, instantly promised relief, which was soon procured, *'for he informed his brother Lochiel of what the alderman had said, and the contributions were greatly abated'.*[58]

It was not until they reached Glasgow that Doctor Archie is mentioned again, this time specifically because of another disagreement with his brother. It was the city of Glasgow itself, or rather the contents of the houses which provoked their quarrel. The houses of the merchants in this rapidly growing town, prospering from foreign trade as ships sailed to and from the River Clyde, contained riches undreamed of by the Highland men. Furniture, porcelain, carpets and hangings, rich enough to dazzle their eyes were all theirs for the taking, or so they had been led to believe. Visions of all that awaited had been one of the few things that kept them going during the last dreary miles of the march. Looting the houses of the conquered was a just reward, a perquisite accepted throughout the ages as one of the rewards of victory. Now it was doubly justified by all that they had endured.

But Archie Cameron, well aware of how the men had suffered, thought otherwise. It was plain to him that they must treat the citizens with humanity if there was any chance of winning them to their cause.

Lochiel found himself in a dilemma. The men and most of their officers were clamouring for what they thought to be their rights. In refusing them he risked rebellion but Archie, patient as ever, eventually brought it home to him that he would lose all credence in the city if he allowed it to be sacked.

It was a brave decision made in the face of fury and derision from most of a body of half starved, exhausted men lusting for the plunder they believed to be almost in their hands. Grumbling and rancour continued amongst the disappointed men. But the people of Glasgow rejoiced.

Afterwards, as Lochiel took the credit, and the bells of the city pealed out in his honour, it was barely remembered that it was the quiet, unassuming doctor, in his by now worn clothes and shabby wig, who had prevailed upon his chief to forbid this time honoured practice of looting.

After a week spent in Glasgow, Prince Charles led his army north to Stirling, along the foot of the Campsie Fells. On the way they went through what was then the hamlet of Kirkintilloch where, some time previously, two of Lady Lochiel's servants had been murdered. The Camerons wanted to sack the place, killing indiscriminately as they went. But again it was Doctor Archie who firmly forbade such bestial behaviour, and the men, respecting his authority, reluctantly obeyed his word.

Chapter 19
FALKIRK

Reaching Stirling the Jacobites failed to take the castle for lack of heavy guns. Soon it became known that General Hawley, sent up from England to take command of the Government troops, was advancing from Edinburgh.

On 17th January Prince Charles' army was drawn up in battle order on the Plean Muir, two miles to the southeast of Bannockburn, scene of Bruce's victory in 1314. So close was it to Falkirk that people climbed up to view the forthcoming battle from the top of the church tower.

It was almost four o'clock in the afternoon, already nearly dark in what was becoming a heavy storm, when Hawley ordered his dragoons to advance. The watchers from the church first saw the English army enter the mist-covered moor at the top of the hill, as gun smoke merged with the dusk. Then, within what seemed to be minutes, they watched in amazement as the English soldiers fled down the slope. Immediately the inhabitants of Falkirk, most of them Jacobites, rushed down to Hawley's camp to begin plundering the stores.

Prince Charles, on perceiving that the greater part of Hawley's troops had fled, put himself at the head of his reserve and advanced towards those who still stood their ground. Lord John Drummond, seeing the Royal Scots in flight, could not believe what was happening. Crying out '*These men behaved admirably at Fontenoy*' he took it to be a feint. Even the Highlanders could not believe what was going on, asking each other in Gaelic '*What is become of the men? Where are they?*' Bewildered, they remained on the battlefield until Prince Charles ordered several detachments, under the command of Lord John Drummond, Lochiel and Lord

George Murray, to enter the town of Falkirk and find out what was taking place. Lord John entered at the west end, Lochiel by a lane near the centre, and Lord George by another further east, called the Cow-Wynd, where they found that the English had just retreated from Falkirk, leaving a few straggling parties in the streets. The Camerons, on emerging from the Cow Wynd *'made prodigious slaughter'* on a group of the enemy soldiers whom they found in the next street.[59] Darkness was increasing, the road so slippery with rain and sleet that the scrimmage taking place within the confines of the houses on either side became a free running battle. As always close behind his brother, Archie saw what might have been mud on his hose, before realizing it was blood. Pulling him to the side of the road, shouting at the men closest to stand around to make a shield, he pulled down the stocking to find the gunshot wound.

It may have been the whiteness of the linen bandage, pulled from the haversack on his back, which caught the marksman's eye. Bending over his brother Archie was thrown backwards by the force of the bullet as it hit the centre of his targe.

The leather, stout enough to lessen the velocity of the impact, saved his life. But, fired at close range, the leaden shot went through it into his chest. Gasping with shock and the pain of what, in the heat of the moment, he probably took to be a minor wound, he staggered to his feet to be carried or supported to a safer place.

Lochiel, his injury bandaged to staunch the blood, led his men onwards in pursuit of the now retreating Hanoverian force. In Hawley's army the number of killed and wounded was estimated at 280 in all. The Jacobite losses were smaller but Doctor Archie's wound proved more serious than either he, or anyone else, had forseen. Extraction of the bullet turned out to be impossible and it remained in his chest, causing him much pain at times, for the rest of his life.[60] Amongst those killed fighting for King George was Sir

Robert Munro of Foulis, a hero of Fontenoy, a man so rotund that he had to remain upright during that battle while his men lay flat to avoid the cannon fire. His brother, an unarmed physician like Doctor Archie, was killed beside him. Later when their bodies were found, by then bare and defaced as to be almost unrecognizable, Sir Robert was still clutching the handle of his sword with a broken blade. Although both Monros were given honourable burial in one grave in the Falkirk cemetery, their clan would long seek revenge on the Jacobites, the Camerons being a prime target, for taking the life of their chief.

That evening, while the Prince lodged in a private house, his army took over the English camp, looting the baggage train and stripping the bodies of the fallen men, leaving them, as described by a citizen of Falkirk, *'like nothing but a large flock of white sheep at rest on the face of the hill'.*[61]

The next day, as the rain continued, the Highlanders collected their spoils. They also buried the dead, employing the country people to dig a large pit in the battlefield into which the bodies were laid. It was while this was happening that a tragic accident occurred, one which was to have a far reaching effect on Doctor Archie for the animosity that it caused.

A private soldier of the Clanranald regiment was cleaning a looted musket. Without realizing that it was double loaded, he extracted what he took to be the only ball, before firing the gun through an open window to clear the powder. By sheer bad luck Aeneas, Young Glengarry, standing on the other side of the street, was mortally wounded by the second shot. Aware that it was an accident he pleaded, with his dying breath, for the soldier's life, ineffectually as it proved, for his clansmen, incensed with rage, dragged the man off to be shot against a wall.

This incident was offset by another, mercifully more amusing than tragic. Prince Charles was talking to

Lord Kilmarnock, when a man was seen coming up the street in the uniform of an English regiment, a musket and bayonet in his hand and a black cockade on his hat. Taking him for an assassin, Lord Kilmarnock rushed out into the street with a loaded pistol, only to be pushed aside by the Camerons, who recognized the supposed English soldier as one of their own in captured gear!

On the following day Prince Charles returned to Stirling to resume the siege of the castle. A battery was constructed of bags of sand and wool and a number of cannon brought to aim at the fortress. General Blakeney, the English governor, however, claiming that he could see the very shoe buckles of the besiegers as they stood behind their entrenchments, returned the fire with such deadly accuracy that many of the Jacobite gunners, including the French piquet's, said to be the best soldiers in the army, were killed.

Realizing then that the attempt to take the castle was hopeless, Lord George Murray, at a council of war, insisted they should march north for Inverness. Prince Charles, so infuriated that he struck his head against the wall, agreed with the greatest reluctance to his general's demand.

The Highland army left Stirling on 1st February 1746, just a day after the Duke of Cumberland, who had travelled from London in four days to take command of the army, left Edinburgh in pursuit. Presented by Lord Hopetoun with a coach and twelve horses, he drove in great splendour up the Canongate and the High Street and then through the Grassmarket to the West Port. To the huge crowd of people who cheered him he turned, waving his hat, saying, *'I am in great haste, my friends, but I believe I shall soon be back to you with good news'.* Settling back with satisfaction against the leather seat of the coach he was unaware that the streets had rung with the cheers of those same people when Prince Charles had left his Scottish capital for England just three calendar months before.

Chapter 20
THE SIEGE OF FORT WILLIAM

On Monday 19th February the Highland army took the town of Inverness. Then, in early March Lochiel, in command of the Camerons, Keppoch Macdonalds, and Stewarts of Appin, marched south-west to besiege the fortress of Fort William, the little town formerly known as Maryburgh, near the confluence of Loch Linnhe and Loch Eil.

Donald made his headquarters in Glennevis from where, on 20th March 1746, he wrote two letters, one to Cluny MacPherson, the other to Prince Charles. His mind was inflamed with fury by the burning of Morvern, carried out only ten days previously, on the positive orders of Cumberland. Troops landed from two government ships had burnt and sacked twenty-four of the little farming townships near the coast over an area of fourteen miles.

Reading Lochiel's letters, one is shocked even today by the hatred of the Campbells that springs from the pages with the force of a clenched fist. The fact that they were acting under orders being to him no excuse. To Cluny *'his dear Cousine'* after describing preparations for the siege, he wrote:

> but what gives me joy in a particular manner is the fate of the Campbells, the plunderers of our countries...As a proof of their hellish design (authorised by their darling Cumberland which I have discovered by a letter from the Sheriff of Argyll to the Governor of Fort William, intercepted by one of my own men) a party of Campbells took the opportunity while the country of Morvine was destitute of men, to burn all the farms upon the coast of it that were inhabited by either Camerons or McLeans – first plundered the houses, strip't the poor women and children, killed all the horses that came in their way and

> even set fire to their byres without allowing them to turn out their cattle, such barbarity was never heard of. There are three hundred and fifty of the Campbells at Fort William - two men of war – they are dayly attempting by their party to land at Corpach, and other farms in Lochiel, to burn and carry of Cattel, but prevented by our guards who have killed some of them, and we expect by tomorrow night to begin cannonading and bombarding of the Fort and hope soon to be master of it – cost what it will.[62]

To the Prince he wrote in the same tone, vowing *'to hang a Campbell for every house that shall hereafter be burnt by them'.*[63] And this from the 'Gentle Lochiel'!

On that same day Lochiel and MacDonald of Keppoch jointly signed a manifesto, which read:

> I cannot omit to giving notice that my people have been the first to have felt the cowardly barbarity of my pretended Campbell friends. I shall only desire to live to have an opportunity of thanking them for itt in the open field.

This document, recorded in the Campbell of Stonefield Manuscript, now in Register House Edinburgh, was also printed in the Scots Magazine for March 1746. Sent to Donald Campbell of Octomore, governor of Castle Stalker, the elderly man on receiving it expressing his surprise at its vehemence.

The letters, in fact, sum up the greatest tragedy of the rebellion in that they re-ignited clan feuding at a time when more enlightened men understood how such vendettas were stripping the country of its wealth. Lochiel, who in his efforts to stop cattle raiding, had proved himself to be one of them, as had his brother Archie, had now been made irrational in his thinking by the mindless savagery shown to his people, for which he blamed the Campbells, it seems to an unfair degree.

General Campbell, the Duke of Argyll's cousin, in command of the army of the North West of Scotland and the Isles, writing to the deputy sheriff, Campbell of Stonefield, had already expressed his horror of Cumberland's order to devastate land owned by rebels. Stonefield agreed with him, telling the Duke that:

> It seems reasonable to wish that this order was not carr'd to execution, till once the rebels were thoroughly dispers'd, and a strong force brought into their country, lest they should fall upon his Majesty's loyall subjects in revenge. ...Men reduced to absolute dispair will attempt any thing.[64]

The Duke was certainly concerned, particularly in view of the fact that Morvern, where so much damage had already been inflicted, was actually his own land. Moreover he agreed with Stonefield that the militia, (local men enlisted in the emergency) should not be used to fight fellow farmers like themselves.

But William Duke of Cumberland, the supreme commander, acting for his father King George II, had to be obeyed.

Aware of the importance of Fort William as '*the only fort in the Highlands that is of any consequence*', he appointed Captain Caroline Scott to supersede the elderly governor, Alexander Campbell, in command,[65] before sending a detachment of Guise's Foot from Edinburgh to reinforce the garrison, already held by three companies of the same regiment. Over and above this, supplied by ships sent from Glasgow to Loch Linnhe, the soldiers were well fed. Lochiel's army was the opposite:

> 'Both the Lochiels' *reported the Duke's factor, Campbell of Auchindoun from Mingary,* 'with all there men and 400 of those they call the French

> are now at Lochaber, in all 17 or 18 hundred. They are in a starveing way tho' I am credibly inform'd that they are making up girnells and other conveniencys for stores at Lochiel's house at Auchanacary *(Achnacarry)* I believe they have the utmost difficulty to bring up there artillery for want of strong horses'.[66]

'God knows' *wrote O'Sullivan afterwards:*

> what peines we had to send them the artillery, ammunition, meal, and even fourgage, for there was not a scrap to be had in that part of the country, the roads were frozen, the horses reduc'd to nothing, and not a carter that knew how to drive or guide them.[67]

Due to the difficulty of moving cannon, the siege did not begin until the 20th. The next day the Jacobites began a cannonade from a battery of 3 guns, throwing about 60 or 70 shells upon the little town, and on the third day they sent a French drummer with a summons to surrender, but he was not allowed into the garrison. On the 27th they stationed a second battery above the Governor's garden, from where his horse was wounded in its stable. On the 29th they established a third battery on the Craigs where, in addition to the 3 brass four pounders, they had a furnace which heated hot bullets, aimed to set buildings on fire.

The roofs of the town were badly damaged and the old barrack building almost destroyed before, on 31st March, Captain Caroline Scott, leading 150 men, marched out of the fort to demolish the battery, capture the cannons and the furnace and thus bring the siege to an end, which he reported triumphantly.

Just three days later Lochiel received instructions to raise the siege and proceed to Inverness, where it was known that the main body of the Highland army, headed by the Duke of Cumberland, was advancing from Aberdeen.

Chapter 21
THE FINAL BATTLE

Doctor Archie is not specifically mentioned in the records of those cold months of late winter, which became an ice bound spring. Possibly his wound was the reason, the skin over the embedded bullet being not properly healed. Otherwise he was more than likely fully occupied in dealing with the many cases of illness amongst the soldiers which are known to have occurred.

The men, largely undernourished and tired from the long march, were prone to influenza and similar winter ills. The Prince himself, in Inverness, fell ill of *'the spotted fever'*, presumably measles or rubella or possibly chicken-pox. He recovered after several days in bed but Murray of Broughton, a frail man with a weaker constitution, was too ill to leave Inverness.

To make matters worse the Prince was now extremely short of money while, at the same time, the cost of food increased. Meal, mainstay of the army, was in very short supply and the purveyors were making a fortune as the officers of the army had to pay for it themselves. The sight of the government army provision ships sailing into the firth added insult to injury in the minds of near starving men, and when Lord George Murray decided that a night march to Nairn would be a good opportunity to surprise Cumberland's soldiers, celebrating their Commander's birthday in the little town only a few miles to the east, they must have wondered how they would manage to summon up the strength to encompass it. In the event they did not, and the march, over impossible ground in the dark, had to be abandoned as the dawn approached. The doubly weary soldiers trailed back to Drumossie Muir and fell where they could to sleep for the few hours left to them before the inevitable battle.

And so, on 16th April, these same Highland soldiers, cold, exhausted and hungry, faced the well fed

Hanoverian army on the desolate Culloden Moor. At about eleven o'clock in the morning the skyline to the east blackened with the troops of the Duke of Cumberland, like the threat of a coming storm.

Colonel O'Sullivan, acting as both adjutant and quartermaster-general, drew up the Prince's army. The men of Lochiel's regiment were placed in the front of the Highland line, the Atholl Brigade to their right, the Stewarts of Appin, the Frasers and the MacIntoshes to their left.

From accounts of similar engagements it would seem that the medical officers of both armies were stationed in tents behind the lines. In this instance, however, Doctor Archie and his colleagues may have made use of what are described as *'a rude farmhouse'* and its outbuildings on the right of the Highland line.[68] Certainly it is known that wounded men were carried to a barn where, following the battle, Cumberland's soldiers stabbed them to death.

Wherever they were positioned, the procedure would have been the same. Trestle tables would have been put up on which men were laid as they were carried in. Knives sharpened by honing would have been placed in readiness for amputations. Bandages and splints, pincers to extract bullets, sponges to staunch blood and above all brandy to relieve the shock and pain, would also have been ready to hand. The doctors themselves would have worn long aprons that soon would be soaked in gore.

The action began at about one o'clock when the Jacobite gunners fired ineffectually over the heads of the Hanoverian king's troops. The men scrugged down their bonnets, as was the custom before a charge, pulling their blue caps low over their foreheads to make them secure. A few moments passed before Colonel Bedford, a skilled engineer, gave orders to return the fire.

The result was devastation. Cannon balls mowed down whole lanes of the Highland infantry standing waiting for the order to charge which did not come. Men fell, screaming in rage and agony among the smoke from the enemy guns. At last Young MacLachlan, a Jacobite for all that he was the son of the Duke of Argyll's captain of Innischonnell Castle on Loch Awe, was sent with a message from the Prince to Lord George Murray to begin the attack. But it never arrived, MacLachlan's head being blown off by a cannon ball as he galloped down the line. The MacIntoshes did not wait for more. Maddened by inaction, they leapt forward, as one man, in a murderous roar.

Lochiel had been talking to Lord George Murray just before some members of the Clan Chattan Confederation, comprising the MacIntoshes, MacGillivrays and Macbeans, backed up by Maclachlans and Macleans, made their tumultuous onslaught. Immediately, as he gave the command, the Camerons followed, their pipers playing their rallying march, and the combined force of the Highlanders broke the Hanoverian line.

But then came the grape shot, the lethal combination of small metal bags or slugs, often with the addition of nails, which on firing spread out like the pellets of a shot gun. Nothing previously devised had been as devastatingly effective against infantry at short range.

Doctor Archie if, as must be presumed, he was somewhere behind the lines, can only have heard the dreadful sounds of battle, his mind being totally focused on coping with the carnage that it caused. That his brother was amongst the casualties was something of which, initially, he was probably unaware.

Fifty yards from the enemy's front line Lochiel, about to draw his sword, was hit in both ankles by grapeshot. Falling forward in agony, he watched his men fighting, as he managed to pull himself upwards by placing his weight on both hands. Without waiting for instruction, some of his Camerons used their own initiative to save their wounded chief, *'two carrying his legs, a third supporting his head, while the rest posted themselves round him as an impregnable bulwark, and in that manner carried him from the field, over the small River Nairn, to a place of safety'.*[69] That Doctor Archie was by then present is verified by Lord Amulree who asserts that *'After the battle of Culloden, Cameron helped his brother, Lochiel, badly wounded in both ankles, off the field'.*[70] This happened almost simultaneously as Prince Charles was himself led from the scene of carnage by Colonel O'Sullivan, with the jibes of Lord Elcho, calling him a cowardly Italian, ringing so cruelly in his ears.

According to the narrative of the Reverend John Cameron, the men who carried Lochiel from the battlefield took him to a little barn, *'where as they were taking off his clothes to disguise him, the barn was surrounded by a party of dragoons'* who nearly took him prisoner. Was this, in fact, the makeshift field hospital? Why otherwise would they have taken him there if not to find his brother, the doctor? The minister does not say so, being too concerned in describing what must have been, for all concerned, a very narrow escape.

Soon, either before or after they crossed the River Nairn, the four Cameron men found a horse for their wounded chief. Supported in the saddle by strong arms, he managed to ride the thirty miles to the newly built house of Lochiel's cousin Cluny MacPherson in Badenoch, beside the great river Spey.

Chapter 22
HUNTED MEN

Meanwhile, on the day of the battle the Prince's secretary, John Murray of Broughton, who had become so dangerously ill in Inverness, had been carried across Loch Ness to Mrs Grant's house of Morriston where, according to his *Memoirs,* he was joined by Doctor Cameron who told him of the disaster at Culloden on the previous day. This would seem to indicate that, while the four trusted Camerons carried their Chief to Lochaber, Archie remained to meet Murray of Broughton on the north side of Loch Ness.

On 18th April Murray was well enough to go on to meet the Duke of Perth at Invergarry. The Duke, by now a very sick man, exhausted and dispirited, having lost all faith in the Rising, gave him little encouragement in his plans to rally the Prince's army.

The *Memoirs* continue to tell how Murray then resolved to continue his journey to Lochiel's country and there wait for accounts of Prince Charles. He was that night carried to Clunes (a house about a mile north of Achnacarry) and from thence the next day to Achnacarry. The following morning he went on to Glen Mallie '*Glenmely, where he had no sooner arrived, than accounts were brought that Lochiel had reached his own house; which occasioned universal joy, his death being reported all over the Country*'.[71] About two hours afterwards Murray arrived at Achnacarry with Stewart of Ardshiel, that enormous man whose providential escape from the battle, where his size had made him hard to miss, was accredited to his being shadowed by his half-brother, the enigmatic Allan Breck, later to become so famous as the supposed assassin of Colin Campbell of Glenure.

There the three of them agreed that they would try to rally a force of men '*who would keep the hills*' till it was discovered whether help was coming from France or not.

Lochiel's joy at being back in his own house, tended to by his brother, can be imagined. But it was not to last. Achnacarry was unsafe. Cumberland, reputedly much offended by Lochiel's refusal to accept an honourable surrender, had given orders that the Camerons must be singled out for exceptionally harsh treatment. No one, not even women and children who resisted, was to be spared. Houses, barns, even the poor thatched cottages of the local people, were to be destroyed. Achnacarry would be a prime target and as scouts came in to report that Redcoats were searching in an ever widening range for survivors of the Jacobite army, Lochiel knew it was little less than madness to remain in a house built for comfort rather than defence.

Having told his servants to bury as much as they could of what was valuable, he left Achnacarry with great sadness guessing, as it proved correctly, that it would soon be sacked before being burnt to the ground.

Two nights after Murray's arrival, both he and Lochiel, who was unable to walk, were carried on the backs of stout ponies up a track beside the river Arkaig to a place called Callich, on the north shore of Loch Arkaig. With them went Doctor Archie, his medical bag holding the salves and bandages with which to treat his brother's wounds also carried by a pony, or else by one of the ghillies who, like himself, went on foot.

Three days later, for greater safety, the whole party crossed the loch by boat to the south shore where, in a thick forest mostly of towering Scots pines, they found some '*little hutts*', hastily put up for the purpose of providing a safe hiding place.[72]

Here someone, presumably a scout, came in with the news that the Prince was in Arisaig. Murray, anxious to persuade him not to leave the country, was desperate to see him, but was too weak from his illness to travel a distance over rough ground, some of it very steep, for nearly thirty miles.

Thus it was Doctor Archie – apparently outwardly recovered from his wound sufficiently to be thought fit enough to go – who was sent with Murray's message to the Prince.

From the map it would seem that he went up Loch Arkaig to Glen Pean before crossing the watershed to Loch Morar from where he may have proceeded by boat. Somewhere in Arisaig he met John Hay of Restalrig, the man who, on Murray's incapacity, had taken over as the Prince's secretary. Hay was elusive, suspiciously so in Archie's opinion, so that when he was told that the Prince would not see him but that he (Hay) would take a message to him, Doctor Archie insisted that he must see the Prince in person. Eventually, after much blustering, Hay told him that he believed that the Prince had in fact already gone. Archie refused to believe him until Hay offered to send someone to find out if what he had been told was true.

The man returned so quickly that he could not possibly have reached the coast. Hay met him out of Archie's hearing which made him suspect that Hay was telling him what to say. The man then assured him that the Prince had sailed some hours before.

Murray still would not believe him when Archie returned with this news. Furious, he wrote a threatening letter to Hay, sending it with a Mr Macleod. But this messenger had only gone half way before he met Hay heading for Loch Arkaig, who assured him that the Prince had indeed gone. He also said that Sir Thomas Sheridan was heading for Lochiel's hiding place by Loch Arkaig as was he himself, and gave him the astonishing news that two French ships, laden with money, arms and ammunition, were lying at anchor in Loch nan Uamh.

Chapter 23
THE FATAL TREASURE

Intelligence sent to Colonel Napier from Scotland about Seven Casks of Money for the Rebels:

> Soon after the battle of Culloden a French privateer anchored in Loch Nonha *(Loch nan Uamh)* in Arisaig, where Doctor Cameron, Brother to Lochiel, Cameron of Dungallon *(Dr Cameron's brother-in-law, later prisoner in Edinburgh Castle)* and many other Rebels were then skulking. One of his Majesties' 20 gun Ships and 2 Sloops were cruising on the West Coast, immediately got intelligence of the privateers, and came up and attacked them, but before the action began they had landed 7 Casks of money and committed it to the charge of Doctor Cameron, who was upon the shore with a great many others of the Camerons and MacDonalds, who flocked from all corners to see the engagement, and among others McDonald of Barrisdale, now prisoner, was also present and Alexd. McLachlan in Lidderdale and Aide-de-Camp to the Pretender.[73]

The ships threw a different light on the chances of those in hiding from the threatened persecution of advancing Hanoverian troops. Murray describes how he and Lochiel *'retired into a little hutt where Lochiel expressed his unwillingness to desert his Clan in the unhappy Situation they were in'.* Saying it was inconsistent with his honour to desert his people, he begged Murray to stay with him *'as them two had gone along hand in hand during the whole affair, they might now share the same fate together'.*[74]

Lochiel's decision was certainly brave though rather, under the circumstances, somewhat foolhardy. Still hardly able to stand, he suggested that one of the ships should sail to Uist where the Prince was thought to be and, if he was not there, it should continue to the Orkneys, where he was most likely to go. Then, to his great relief, old Sir Thomas Sheridan, who was in fact his *bête noir*, said that he would seize at the opportunity of sailing back to France.

Sheridan went with instructions to find out what had happened to all the Spanish money sent to further the Prince's cause and which, amounting to six or seven hundred pounds, was held in Aeneas MacDonald the Banker's possession, telling him to send it, which he did.

More urgently, the men in the huts by Loch Arkaig found themselves faced with the problem of what to do with the huge amount of French money lying in the holds of the waiting ships. Naturally, it was feared that the French Commodore and his officers would be most unwilling to part with it when they found that the Prince had gone.

It was in this state of emergency that Major Kennedy and Doctor Archie set out at night to tell the French officers that Murray was on his way to collect the money, as in fact happened next day.

Kennedy and Doctor Archie arrived at Keppoch, opposite the bay where the French ships, the *Mars* and the *Bellona* lay at anchor, having fended off the three British men-of-war which had attacked them. At sight of the enemy approaching, they had landed the money, consisting of thirty-five thousand *Louis d'ors* in seven casks, which had all been hastily hidden in a wood. In the confusion, however, one of the casks disappeared. Two men were arrested for theft, but reputedly it was found with only one bag of money missing, by a boy aged eight, even as the Court Martial of the supposed two thieves was taking place.

This was only the first unfortunate incident concerning the money, which was to cause so much dispute among families and eventually prove a deciding factor in Doctor Archie's death. Immediately Coll

MacDonald of Barrisdale, having already purloined everything he could lay his hands on, and Young Clanranald, demanded that the money be divided between them in recompense for their losses. Murray, to keep them quiet, agreed to pay not only their arrears of army payment, but gave half a *Louis d'or* to each wounded man and also a consideration to the widows. Having settled the matter in this way, he sent off the money under Doctor Cameron's care. His men carried the barrels for three miles over the hills to Loch Morar, where they loaded it into a boat. Murray, who was following, on reaching the island in Loch Morar, was told that some of Clanranald's men had tried to grab the gold from Doctor Archie but that '*partly by threats and flattery'* he had safely brought it to his Chief.

The report sent to the Duke of Cumberland by his *Aide-de-camp* Colonel Napier, making free use of capital letters, gives a vivid description of the hiding of the gold:

> And having dismissed all the Country people He *(Doctor Archie)* with Major Kennedy, a french Officer *(Sir Stuart Threipland?)* and Alexd. Mcleod, son to Mr John McLeod advocate, took the money out of the Casks, and put it underground in the head of Locharkick, in the middle of a Wood.
>
> There was £6 or 7,000 sterling in each Cask, All put up in separate bags, £1000 in Each bag. They afterwards carried away the empty Casks and where at a considerable distance themselves (none being present but the 3 persons above named) from the place where the Money was hid, They caused the Country people to put them under ground in a different place in order to deceive.
>
> After this was over, All persons were employed to enquire after the cask that was stole during the engadgement. And by the assistance and authority of a priest *(Father Harrison)* who is

great in that country *(all Roman Catholics)* the money was recovered except £700, and that is still missing. *(An Irishman confessed to the priest that he had stolen it but it was never recovered).* His Majestie's troops afterwards search'd the woods of Locharkick for this money, and were often round the hiding place where it was, and missed very narrowly finding it, for being hid by Gentlemen, not used to work, it was very unskilfully done, and the stamps and impressions of their feet visible about the place. But as soon as Doctor Cameron found a proper opportunity, He went and took up the money and hid it in two different places of the wood. In one of them he put 12,000 l., which he shewed to his own son, and another man, That in case he was taken it might not be lost altogether, and the other part he put in a place which he shewed to nobody.[75]

Chapter 24
GOLD FOR GUNS

Two days after Archie's return to Loch Arkaig with the gold he, with his brother Lochiel, as well as Murray and the other men who had been living in the huts, moved about three miles down the north shore of Loch Arkaig to Mortleg, where a rendezvous of the chiefs, meeting to discuss plans for a renewed summer campaign, was arranged. It was Doctor Archie who said that *'The ships from France resolved them to go again to arms'.*[76]

First to appear was Lord Lovat, carried by his ghillies from Castle Dounie which, from a hilltop, he had then seen burnt to the ground. He was followed by Gordon of Glenbucket, John Roy Stewart, Clanranald, Lochgarry, Barrisdale and others. Murray proposed that an obligation should be signed by the persons there present not to desert one another which Lovat, saying that he could put no force into the field, refused to sign. Murray then promised to produce cattle to feed the army and to have a sufficient number of horses at the head of Loch Sheil to carry the ammunition, on the proviso that Clanranald would let it be brought through his country, to which he reluctantly agreed.

It was then settled that the forces would congregate at Glen Mallie, on the south side of Loch Arkaig, three miles from Achnacarry, after which the meeting broke up.

Lord Amulree records that the accounts kept for Murray of Broughton show that it was Doctor Archie who supplied the beef to feed the little army gathering near Loch Lochy in early May. Item 8 reads as follows:

> Mr M. paid Mrs Cameron about £40 for part of their cattle in the Doctor's presence, the others he cannot recall to mind being country people.

The cattle bought from Doctor Cameron and others to supply men rendezvoused at Glenmely £90.

Item 9. Doctor Cameron was the person Mr M. chiefly employed to procure their horses and some of these were bought from a tenant of Lochiel's in Glenpean.

The horses to carry the ammunition to be sent by Mr MacDonald of Clanranald from the coast of Arisaig to the head of Loch Shiel. £45.[77]

1. Sir Ewen Cameron of Lochiel 1629 - 1719

2. Donald Cameron 'The Gentle Lochiel' 1695 - 1748

3. The Scots College was a centre of Jacobitism from 1688 - 1746

4. The hill above Loch Sheil that is the most likely to be the site of the raising of the Standard.

5. Ancient barn at Glenfinnan used for storage of arms and gunpowder.

6. Near the foot of Loch Lochy where the Camerons mustered for the 1745 rising.

7. The Beech Avenue by the River Arkaig 'sheuched' in hurriedly by The Gentle Lochiel.

8.The ruins of Old Achnacarry burned down 28th May 1746

9. Loch nam Uamh scene of the final departure.

10. Ben Nevis from across Loch Lochy

11. The head of Loch Arkaig

12. Murlaggan Bay

13. The ruins of Tigh na Saighdearan

Chapter 25
A COUNTRY ON FIRE

A few days later the rally of the clans proved a great disappointment to Lochiel. Only 200 Camerons, a few Macleans, and 120 MacDonalds under Barrisdale turned up. Together with his brother and Murray he waited two days, but as many deserted as appeared. MacDonald of Lochgarry eventually came, but bringing only 100 instead of the 400 he had promised, and of Lovat there was never a sign.

Lochiel, resilient as ever, was preparing to cross the river Lochy with his little force, when he was told that a party of Munro's, thirsting for blood since their defeat at Falkirk, where their chief had been killed, was approaching from the further bank.

At the same time Major-General Bland, in command of Fort Augustus, was marching down the Great Glen, while Lord Loudoun was aiming to come over the hills to take Achnacarry in a pincer move. Loudoun fortunately was late, giving Lochiel just enough time to move his force up the north side of Loch Arkaig from where he dismissed his men.

From the top of the loch, as Murray reported, they could see the whole country on fire. Achnacarry was known to be occupied by soldiers. On Saturday 22nd May, Colonel Howard of the Buffs, reporting to General Bland that the march over the hills had been the most exhausting he had ever made, told him '*but we are now in Lochyell's house where we are going to dinner... Yesterday I demolished everything before me, but it was not much*'.[78]

Soon, as Lochiel foresaw, the great wooden house built by his grandfather would succumb to the soldiers' flames.

The devastation of the countryside, as described by the minister of Kilmallie, is almost incomprehensible to the modern mind. As always in warfare, especially civil war, it was the innocent who suffered most. Even the Duke of Argyll was horrified to learn that once again militiamen, soldiers called up in the emergency, had been landed from warships, this time to subdue his tenants in Sunart. Nonetheless, concerned as he appears to have been, he did nothing to prevent the devastation that was continuing to take place. Cattle were driven away, houses burnt and men, women and children, including the aged and infirm, driven to take refuge in the hills. Worse still, as the minister wrote, *'they killed several persons in cold blood'.*[79]

Lochiel, in his present predicament, with nothing for it but to go into hiding, found refuge on a little island in Loch Sheil, *Eilean Mhic Dhomhnuill Dhuibh,* Lochiel's Island (lit. the island of the son of Black Donald).

Then, on 30th May, it was learned that Major-General Campbell, in command of the West Highland Army, had landed at Strontian, on Loch Sunart, from where search parties for Jacobites in hiding would soon be combing the hills.

Strontian was Doctor Archie's country. Every one of the miner's families for whom he cared as a doctor was known to him, as was every detail of the land.

That Jean, his wife, was then in Glen Hurich, is proved by Murray's *Memoir.* He describes how, having crossed the ferry on the River Sheil, he went next morning to Glen Hurich to try to get news of Lochiel, and

> having learnt that he was at a farm about seven miles from thence upon the side of Loch Shiel, he went to him and returned the same night to Glenhurick, where, being informed that General Campbell was expected at Strontian...he went two miles higher up the country, where he met with his wife and Mrs Cameron, who had left Strontian a little before the troops landed.

According to another account:

> On hearing the news that General Campbell and Captain Caroline Scott were about to land in the village, they *(Jean Cameron and Margaret Murray)* fled and climbed the hill behind Strontian making for Glen Hurich.

At the same time Lochiel and his party, which included Doctor Archie and Sir Stuart Threipland, had moved for greater security to an island on Loch Sheil. *(this is just off the south bank a few miles from the foot of the loch and is still marked on the O/S map as Lochiel's Island).*

The decision was now taken – by whom we cannot know – that Dungallon would make for Strontian and surrender to General Campbell. The ruse – for ruse it almost certainly was – worked, and the Government forces moved towards Moidart rather than Loch Sheil-side. Campbell questioned Dungallon and received polite responses to all his questions.... Except the locations of the ladies and Lochiel's party.

More factually, it is recorded that Major Alexander Cameron, who had been Prince Charles' standard bearer, had already surrendered to the Government at Fort William, thus hoping that his family's house and property might be spared from the ravages of marauding troops that everywhere was taking place.

Murray does not disclose how his wife, who as far as is known had not followed his wanderings, certainly since he left Inverness, turned up in such a remote part of the Highlands. She was with him in Edinburgh, where the Prince held court before marching for England at the beginning of November, because that is where the child she was now carrying, last of the five which she bore him, must have been conceived.

Margaret, daughter of Colonel Robert Ferguson of Carloch in Nithsdale, a woman noted for her beauty, was at that time *'big with child'*. Murray, her husband, was trying to find a boat to take her to Ireland, unsuccessfully as it seems. According to himself, he gave *'part of the money he had brought from Lochiel, to such as he thought had most occasion for it'*. This must have included Margaret, for somehow she found her way to Edinburgh, where she gave birth to a boy who, unsurprisingly under the circumstances, lived only a few days. Eventually she would leave Murray while, as will be seen later, he was held a prisoner in London.

In the meantime Murray left his wife after having completed financial arrangements for her, and set out in company with Major Kennedy for the place where he had left Lochiel the day before. He entrusted his ailing nephew, Sir David Murray, to Doctor Cameron's care, it having been agreed to send him to a Gentleman's house of the name of Campbell, (Campbell of Ardslignish) where it was imagined he would be safe.

This would prove that Doctor Archie was in Strontian at the end of May, for he had joined his brother on the island in Loch Sheil, but with General Campbell's soldiers only a day's march away, this was no longer safe. Somehow Lochiel was carried, either on horseback or else in the arms of strong men, to Loch Linnhe on the coast of Ardgour. Here they found a boat, sent there by Stewart of Ardshiel, himself now living in a cave, in which Lochiel, with his brother and Murray and a few companions, was rowed up Loch Linnhe and into Loch Leven, near Ballachulish.

Chapter 26
CAPTURE AND ESCAPE

General Campbell, who had sailed from Dunstaffnage to Tobermory in a tender called the *Charles,* put back to the mainland to land at Strontian on 28th May. On 31st, in a letter to General Faulkner, he told him of the treasure landed in Loch nan Uamh which had now mysteriously disappeared. He then described how Alexander Cameron of Dungallon:

> wrote me a letter offering to surrender, a copy of which I send you, and in the evening came in and deliver'd up his own arms and desir'd I would allow him to send around the country and call in such as depended on him to do the same, in consequence of which several are come in, and have brought the best arms I have seen, some belonging to His Majesty's troops and some Spanish. He seems a bashful modest man, extremely sensible of his crime, and gives a very ingenuous and satisfactory answer to such questions as I have ask'd him.[80]

On 9th June Dungallon and Old Glencoe were sent to Inveraray under an armed guard. The General, concerned lest they be treated badly by men such as Captain Fergussone, but at the same time taking no chances, wrote to sheriff Campbell of Stonefield on their behalf, *'I beg you will order them to be well used but when they goe abroad that an officer may attend them. Such letters as are directed to them and such as they write ought to be looked into'.*[81]

It was shortly after this that a detachment of Brigadier Houghton's regiment reached Achnacarry where, finding the house burnt to ashes, they began searching for the plate and other things of value which they rightly guessed had been hidden somewhere in the grounds. The whole place was deserted but eventually they found a gardener whom they seized and questioned as to where the Cameron family's possessions were hidden. He pretended total ignorance, upon which they *'tied him to two halberts and lashed him on the naked back with rods, till the smart forced him to discover the place of concealment, where they found the hidden treasure'.* Then letting him go they told him to inform his master of what had occurred and what he saw and suffered.[82]

Lochiel had left his island hideout on Loch Sheil just in time. Some ten miles away to the north-west, by Loch Morar, Lord Lovat was less fortunate. The frigate H.M.S. *Furnace,* commanded by Captain John Fergussone, was anchored off the shore and, believing that Lord Lovat was in hiding on an island in the loch, he posted men all around to prevent any chance of escape. But Lovat had fled the island before Fergussone's troops arrived. Destroying the island Seminary while they were about it, they later found Lovat hiding in a hollow tree at Meoble on the south side of Loch Morar. Too corpulent and arthritic to walk, *'he was put into a litter, and the soldiers made a run with him to the sea-side, the pipers playing Lovat's march, with which he seemed well pleased'.*[83] Thus, defiant of disaster, he was carried a prisoner to the ship.

In spite of their own great danger of capture Lochiel and Archie, together with Murray, remained near Ballachulish for a week. North of the mouth of Loch Leven was Cameron land, yet discovery might have happened at any moment, the garrison at Fort William being only about sixteen miles away. Nonetheless Lochiel, convinced that the Prince was coming, was determined to take the risk.

A message from Prince Charles had reached him, while still on Loch Arkaig, saying that he had failed to find a ship to take him to France and asking for his help. Lochiel had sent two men across the Minch to look for him and waited, sometimes hopefully, sometimes in near desperation, for what he prayed would be their return.

It was from Loch Leven that Murray of Broughton decided to make a run for it, trying to get to Leith where skippers friendly to the Jacobites could be bribed to cross the North Sea, or to his Border home. Setting off in darkness, he was rowed to the head of the loch before making for Glen Lyon. The reason for this being that his sister, supposedly going there to drink goat's milk, would be able to tell him where it was safe to travel and also whom he could trust.

Archie Cameron went with him only as far as Glen Lyon, this being the last reference made of him in Murray's loquacious *Memoirs*. From Glen Lyon Murray went on to Polmood, the house of another sister in Lanarkshire where, falling into bed exhausted, he was woken at two in the morning by dragoons hammering on the door. Taken prisoner to Edinburgh, he was later transferred to the Tower of London and, by turning King's evidence, he secured the execution of Lord Lovat in return for his own pardon.

Chapter 27
BEN ALDER

The cessation of his name in Murray's *Memoirs* throws a blank period over the life of Doctor Archie from the last week of June, when they parted, until the 20th of August. He may have returned from Glen Lyon to join his brother near Loch Leven for a time, or perhaps it was now that he returned to the Ardnamurchan Peninsula to check on the welfare of his wife and family as it was believed that he did during the summer of 1746.

Batchelor's Hall, his house at Strontian, had been burnt to the ground. Farther north in Glenkingie, his herds of cattle were either slaughtered, or driven away. If Jean was living with her mother in Glenhurich as, from what Murray wrote, would seem to have been the case, he must have gone there in secret, probably on nights without a moon. That he was in hiding nearby, however, is suggested by an anonymous writer who, after admitting that:

> While I have come across no evidence to show that Dr Archibald's wife resided in Ardnamurchan at any time during the '45 and subsequent to her going abroad, there is a possibility that she had been staying with her mother at Glenhurich. The fact that I have come across the statement that one of their younger children died in Ardnamurchan lends some support to such a belief. That the Doctor did himself, when a fugitive after Culloden, find a refuge in the peninsula cannot be ruled out for there is in Northern Ardnamurchan a place known as *'Leabha falaich am Dotair MacDhomhuill Duibh'* 'The Hiding Bed of the Doctair MacDonald Dubh' *(MacDonald Dubh is the patronymic of Lochiel).*[85]

Did Archie risk going back to Sunart because somehow a message had reached him that one of his children was ill? It is known that during the year of 1746 two of them died of causes unknown. There may have been an epidemic of measles or smallpox, such deadly killers in those days. They may have had tuberculosis and the fact that a daughter called Bel died later of a wasting illness suggests this as a cause. Otherwise, driven from their home to some remote place of hiding, their small bodies weakened by shortage of food, they may have perished from exposure.

If Archie was in Ardnamurchan during part of July, it was probably he who sent word to Lochiel that their brother the priest, Father Alexander, had been taken prisoner in Morar.

First held in the hold of a warship, mastered by a Captain McNeil, Alexander had been transferred to the *Furnace,* a vessel abhorred throughout the Highlands for the bestiality of its commander Captain Fergussone, a man who, while raiding the islands, had become renowned for giving quarter to none. General Campbell, aware of his character, had specifically ordered that Flora MacDonald, another prisoner on the ship, be used with special care. It is doubtful if Father Alexander, held in squalid conditions in the hold, ever saw her, unless he was allowed, as were some of the prisoners, to take exercise on deck.

Father Alexander's brothers, at that time, may not have been aware of the ill treatment which was worsening his already frail health. All that they probably knew was that he had been taken prisoner, but knowledge of Fergussone's reputation must have made them fear for his life.

Lochiel, undoubtedly on horseback because of his injured ankles, risked riding into the wild and largely uninhabited land of the Moor of Rannoch where, by great good fortune, he came across his cousin Cluny MacPherson. Cluny, like him chief of his clan, took him to a shieling on Mullach Coire an Iubhar, on the west side of the Ben Alder Range.

The shieling was typical of the huts of rough stone, built to house the women and children who, during the summer months herded cows on the hills. The roofs of heather or turf were renewed, or patched up, every year. Lochiel, whose wedding contract had included the installation of water closets into Achnacarry, now had nothing but water from a burn and slept on layers of heather to keep the damp from the ground – that is when he slept at all. Men on the mountain, always on the verge of wakefulness, listened for the cry of a bird, the scrunch of boots on stone, which might mean the approach of soldiers sent out from Fort Augustus to search for rebels in the hills.

It is thanks to the memoirs kept by Sir Stuart Threipland, the other doctor who, beside his brother shared Lochiel's place of hiding on Ben Alder, that it is known how Lochiel was kept aware of the terrible sufferings of the people in Lochaber. Threipland, scandalized by what he heard was happening, gave five pounds to help them, saying that if he was short of money he at least knew where to get more, while these poor creatures had nothing at all, a remark taken by some to mean that he had knowledge of the buried gold. As he did so Lochiel himself, made speechless with remorse on hearing of the misery for which he held himself responsible, emptied his purse.

Chapter 28
THE PRINCE SAVED

It was on 5th July, almost as Father Alexander Cameron was taken prisoner, that Prince Charles, after escaping from Benbecula to Skye and from thence to Raasay, reached the mainland of Scotland, landing secretly, possibly at Stoul or Tarbert, some way inland along the south shore of Loch Nevis.

From there he wandered the country, sleeping in the open, or wherever he could find shelter in caves and amongst trees. On 15th August, in pouring rain, he reached the east end of Loch Arkaig, where a message came from Cameron of Clunes, asking him to meet him in a nearby wood. There they were joined by MacDonald of Lochgarry, with whom Charles moved into a small hut '*built for the purpose*' similar to, or perhaps even one of those which, only four months before in April, had been so hastily put up for Lochiel.

By then, through the network of his spies, men whom he knew he could trust, Lochiel had become aware of the whereabouts of the Prince. Robert Chambers describes how Lochiel despatched MacDonald of Lochgarry and Doctor Cameron:

> to learn what they could concerning him...well acquainted with the passes they made their way in safety to the north of the lakes, and very soon met *(Cameron of Clunes)* who told them he would conduct them to the object of their search. Charles was at this moment sleeping on the hill with one of Clune's sons, while Peter Grant held watch. Grant happened to nod upon his post and did not perceive the approaching party till they were very near. He instantly flew to awaken the sleepers. The party had a formidable appearance for, besides Clunes, Lochgarry, and Dr Cameron, there were two servants; and at a little distance they looked like armed militia.

> Grant and young Clunes counselled an immediate flight to the top of the hill in the face of the enemy; but Charles resolved rather to keep close behind the loose stones amidst which they were skulking, and to fight the enemy in ambuscade...*'I am a good marksman'* he said *'and can charge quick. I am therefore sure to do some execution'*....Then he took out a brace of pistols which he had not previously shown, and expressed a hope to make these serviceable in a close struggle...Grant acceded to a resolution so much in unison with his own dauntless spirit, and they had presented their muskets along the stones, and were almost on the point of firing, when fortunately the peculiar form of Clunes was distinguished in the party, which assured them they had nothing to fear. Joy immediately took the place of desperation, and Charles could not help returning thanks to Heaven for having prevented him from destroying so many dear friends. His satisfaction was increased by receiving a message from his beloved friend Lochiel, for whose recovery, of which the Doctor informed him, he thrice audibly thanked the Deity.[85]

Doctor Archie, his own clothes torn and dirty after living so long in the hills, was nonetheless shocked at the sight of Prince Charles, as he wrote afterwards:

> He was then barefooted, had an old black kilt coat on, a plaid, philabeg and waistcoat, a dirty shirt and a long red beard, a gun in his hand, a pistol and dirk by his side. He was very cheerful and in good health, and, in my opinion, fatter than when he was in Inverness.[86]

The doctor and Lochgarry, as they neared the Prince's hideout, had scented roasting meat. Reaching him as he laid aside his pistols, he told them that on the previous day the men with him had killed a cow. The dinner they had that evening, on the mountain top as dusk was drawing in, was one that those who shared it would never afterwards forget. Charles himself ate very heartily *'and enjoyed himself over the novel luxury of some bread, which had been procured for his use from Fort William'.*

He was anxious to cross the chain of mountains and join Lochiel, but this was thought too dangerous because the newspapers had recently reported that he had gone *'over Corryarrack with Lochiel and thirty men'* which would undoubtedly occasion a vigilant search in those parts...

> In the meantime Doctor Cameron ventured into Lochaber to procure intelligence, and Lochgarry posted himself upon the isthmus, between the west end of Loch Lochy and the east end of Loch Linnhe, to watch the motions of the troops.[87]

It was on 20th August that Archie returned to his brother, instructed by the Prince to get his views on the chances of a renewed offensive which Lochgarry believed to be viable. Archie came back to tell Prince Charles that his brother was *'still suffering too much from his wounds to be able to travel',* and then to give him the news that he least wanted to hear, that Lochiel believed a renewed rising to be almost impossible.

Charles, to whom this was just another disappointment, although greatly discouraged decided, with much reluctance, to abandon the whole idea. That he was still in great danger was proved when, a few days later, *'as he was sleeping on the mountainside, with his few remaining attendants, he was roused at eight in the morning by a child who exclaimed she saw a body of red-coats'.* Looking down he saw a troop of soldiers demolishing the huts (another indication that they were those built for Lochiel) and searching the surrounding woods.

There was no time to be lost. Charles and his followers scrambled up the hill, using the dry path of a burn to keep out of sight. From there they managed to reach the top of a hill called Mullantagart, where they stayed all day without food. In the evening a son of Cameron of Clunes appeared to say that his father would meet them at a given place. Charles set out to find it over ground covered with rocks and stumps of trees until, fit as he was, he became so exhausted that only the strong arms of the men with him kept him on his feet.

Mercifully, with Charles staggering between them, they at last found Clunes and another of his sons, *'with a cow which they had killed and partly dressed'*. Saved thus from death by starvation, Charles stayed with them a few days until Lochgarry and Doctor Cameron arrived with the welcome news that *'the passes were not now so strictly guarded and that they might safely venture at least a stage nearer to Lochiel'.*[88]

Lochiel, in the shieling on Mullach Coire an Iubhar, had with him Sir Stuart Threipland, Alan Cameron, his principal servant and two of Cluny's men. Knowing that there was a party of militia stationed only four or five miles away they were all constantly on the alert. Seeing a party of five armed men in Highland dress climbing the hillside towards them, who they thought to be soldiers, Lochiel at once ordered the men with him to load all their guns. The weapons primed, they were just about to fire them from a range at which they could hardly have missed when, struck by something familiar about one of them he recognized his brother Archie and, unbelievably, to one side of him a wild looking figure who, despite his beard and long hair, he knew to be the Prince.

The re-union was utterly joyful. Lochiel, hobbling forward and then stumbling, was trying to kneel before him as Charles told him to rise. Touching him on the shoulder he said:

> Oh no, my dear Lochiel; we do not know who may be looking at us from yonder hills; and, if they see any such motions, they will immediately conclude that I am here.[89]

Lochiel then took him into the little hut where, to his utter amazement, he found a better store of food than any he had seen since Drummossie Muir. There was plenty of mutton, some good beef sausages which had been preserved in a peatbog, the refrigerator of the day, butter and cheese and a large well-cured bacon ham. Best of all there was an anker of whisky and the first thing he called for was a dram, which he drank to the health of all present. Some minced collops were then dressed for him with butter, in a large saucepan which Lochiel and Cluny always carried about with them and which was the only cooking vessel they had. *'Now gentlemen I live like a prince'* Charles cried, as he devoured the collops straight out of the pan with a silver spoon.

Well fed and cheered by the good company, Charles became a different man from the one who had lain almost dying from cold and hunger on the mountain top only two days before. The lacerations on his arms and legs, resulting from that wild scramble in near darkness, were healing (no doubt cleaned and dressed by Doctor Archie) and exhausted, he slept for many hours.

Then Cluny MacPherson, who had gone to Achnacarry to look for him and found him gone, returned. He too would have knelt to Charles, but even as he was bending the Prince took him in his arms and kissed him saying *'I am sorry Cluny, you and your regiment were not at the battle of Culloden;*

I did not hear till lately that you were so near us on that day'.[90]

Prince Charles would have stayed longer but Cluny, saying it was dangerous to do so insisted that they moved to another shieling, called Uischilra which, although filled with smoke when a fire was lit, was safer by its remoteness than the one they had just left behind. Charles grumbled continuously at the discomfort but, with no alternative, endured it for forty-eight hours until, on Cluny's insistence waiting until near darkness, they once again moved on.

Chapter 29
THE HAGGIS

Edging their way across the hillside, constantly on the alert, they reached the amazing edifice, made famous in Stevenson's *Kidnapped,* known as Cluny's Cage. Cluny's own description brings it clearly to the reader's mind:

> It was situated in the face of a very rough, high and rocky mountain called Letternilich, a part of Benalder, full of great stones and crevices, and some scattered wood interspersed. The house was built within a small thick bush of wood. There were first some rows of trees laid down, in order to form a floor for the habitation; and as the place was steep, this raised the lower side to an equal height with the other; and these trees, in the ways of joists or planks, were levelled with earth and gravel. There were betwixt the trees, growing naturally on their own roots, some stakes fixed in the earth, which, with the trees, were interwoven with ropes, made of heath and birch twigs, up to the top of the cage, it being of a round or oval shape; and the whole thatched or covered with fof (moss). This whole fabric hung, as it were by a large tree, which relined from the one end, along the roof, to the other, and which gave it the name of the Cage. By chance there happened to be two stones at a small distance from one another, in the side next the precipice, resembling the pillars of a chimney, where the fire was placed. The smoke had its vent out here, all along the face of the rock, which was so much of the same colour, that one could discover no difference in the clearest day. The Cage was no larger than to contain six or seven persons; four of whom were frequently employed in playing at cards, one idle looking on, one baking, and the other firing bread and cooking.[921]

Sir Stuart Threipland was one of the cooks, as Chambers, in his history of that family, gives an amusing account. Sir Stuart, or Doctor Threipland, as he was more generally known, had evidently inherited his interest in food from his mother, authoress of two books of recipes for which she was much acclaimed. Chambers, recalling what by his time had become a legend, gives a description of what occurred.

He used a recipe he had learned in France with apples, not a usual ingredient, being a main feature of the dish. How he came across the apples in that wild stretch of moorland is not known. It is easy to imagine that Prince Charles, eager for some diversion in the crowded confines of Cluny's Cage, was intrigued with the preparation. We can picture him watching as the chopped liver, oatmeal mixed with blood, and the apples were packed into a sheep's stomach, which Threipland then stitched up, presumably using both thread and needle from his own, or Doctor Archie's medical bag.

The haggis was immersed in a cauldron, hanging from a hook driven into the rock face above the fire. The scent of its cooking, sweetened by the tang of apples, sharpened the appetites of hungry men awaiting the forthcoming feast.

Drawing back to give him room, they held their breaths in excitement as Threipland lifted the haggis onto a wooden plate. Then cries of joy became howls of dismay as, catching his toe on an untrimmed log, he sent the haggis flying from the mouth of the cave to explode in a myriad of pieces on a rock below. Threipland wrote later '*that it would have been amusing had they not been robbed of the dinner which, in that rock bound fastness, would have been better than a banquet in any palace of a king*'.

The debacle of the haggis and the card playing proved to be the only light hearted diversions in days that were otherwise filled with anxiety, awaiting word of the arrival of ships or of any other means by which the Prince and his companions could escape.

Doctor Archie, having stayed at the Cage for a week, then left to take Cluny MacPherson to Loch Arkaig to show him where the gold was buried. Heading north from Ben Alder they crossed a wild track of moorland, deserted except for wild deer and some fortunately undiscovered cattle grazing on the *airidhs* (the high pastures).

Using the natural cover of rocks and beds of burns, they moved largely in the evening and by the light of dawn. Always with eyes on the hillsides, watching for any sign of movement which might warn of military patrols, they went cautiously, the more so when, leaving the high ground, they dropped down into Glen Spean.

There they saw desolation that shocked them to the very roots of their souls. Cottages and barns stood open to the sky, bare walls left blackened by flames that had spread from the thatch of straw and turf set alight by the torches of the redcoats, forced to obey the orders of the Duke of Cumberland. Archie and Cluny, Highlanders both to the core, found themselves bewildered and revolted by what seemed to them the needless cruelty inflicted on people for whom life was hard enough at all times, let alone the present when, left without even their cattle and few possessions, they faced the inevitable hardship of the coming winter months.

Reaching Loch Arkaig, having found the place where the treasure was hidden and made sure that it was safe, they were making their way back to Ben Alder when they came across a runner who was looking for the Prince, to tell him that two French ships were swinging at anchor in Loch nan Uamh, waiting to take him back to France.

The man was one of the line of messengers, stationed by Clan Donald at various points, from

Clanranald's island of South Uist to his mainland district of Moidart, and from thence to the Camerons' country. Returning to Ben Alder, moving mostly at night over paths known to few people other than Cluny, hiding amongst rocks and trees during the day, they returned safely to the Cage.

As Archie broke the news to his brother, he found himself disbelieved. Ships would not come from France as late as September so Donald was convinced. Knowing that they had nothing more than an old atlas from the time of Louis XIV, he believed they would never risk getting lost or wrecked on the treacherous west coast. Also, for all he knew, Commodore Smith's squadron was still searching the sea lochs. The French sea captains, renowned for their sagacity would, he felt certain, never expose their ships and their crews to such risk.

But, on 13th September, on a clear morning when mist was rising from Loch Ericht, Captain John MacDonald, brother of Glenaladale, appeared at the cave to confirm the news that two French ships were indeed lying in Loch nan Uamh.

From the head of Glenaladale, which opens into Loch Sheil, it was only about four miles to Loch Ailort, the sea loch on the south side of the peninsular of Ardnish to the north of which lies Loch nan Uamh. Wounded three times at Culloden, Alexander MacDonald of Glenaladale, a major in Clanranald's Regiment, had posted spies to watch for the first sign of coming sails. He now sent off a message to his brother John, telling him to inform the Prince of the ships reaching Loch nan Uamh.

John MacDonald, Alexander's younger brother, who had last seen Prince Charles at the east end of Loch Arkaig from whence he had gone to try to find Lochiel, returned there only to find him gone. Moving east in the general direction of Cluny's Cage, (actually some twenty six miles east of Achnacarry) he came across a poor local woman who gave him directions to the Cage, still some eight miles away, but further over the circuitous route that he must take to avoid the search parties from the garrisons of Fort William and Fort Augustus, known to be still scouring the hills.

Told by John MacDonald of the ships lying at anchor the Prince, together with Lochiel, Cluny and MacDonald of Lochgarry, set off across the steep slopes from Ben Alder, heading due west for Loch nan Uamh.

The first night they spent in the smoky bothy of Uischilra where they were joined by John Roy Stewart and MacPherson of Breakachie, who had brought with him three of the Prince's gold and silver mounted pistols. *'it is remarkable'* Charles said as they were handed to him *'that my enemies have not discovered one farthing of my money, a rag of my cloaths, or one piece of my arms'.*[92]

Next day on they went, by this time so jubilant that they are said to have taken pot shots at their bonnets, flinging them in the air!

Heading north between Ben Alder and the west side of Loch Ericht they walked towards Glen Roy before, on reaching the River Lochy, they found themselves stranded on the bank. Cameron of Clunes then appeared in a patched up leaky old boat. On inspection, Lochiel recognized it as one of his own which the soldiers, providentially, had failed to find and burn. Clunes then produced six bottles of brandy, which he claimed to have stolen from the garrison at Fort Augustus. All of them, immediately, took not one but several drams, accounting for three of the bottles in a remarkably short time. Their spirits much emboldened they took to the little boat, Clunes going first, then the Prince, then Lochiel. Somehow during the ferrying, the remaining three bottles of brandy were broken, the liquor mixing with the water sloshing about at their feet. The boatmen drank it happily, once their passengers were safely on the shore!

Walking stealthily, largely in the dusk or first light, they reached Achnacarry on the night of 16th September. The ruined house, the timbers still reeking of fire, was an awful, heartbreaking sight to Lochiel.

Hateful as it was to him, they stayed there for the next day confident that, because of its ruination, the soldiers who had already taken everything of value would not return. Leaving as darkness descended, casting a merciful shroud over the stark ruined walls, they reached the head of Loch Arkaig the following day. There, to their great joy, they found Cluny MacPherson and Doctor Archie, who had gone on ahead, cooking both meat and bannocks, a meal which despite his despair over Achnacarry, Lochiel heartily enjoyed.

From there, on 19th September, after another day's walk, they reached Borrodale, to see before them the two French privateers. The larger vessel, aptly named *L'Heureux*, carrying thirty guns, and crewed by three hundred men, and the smaller, the *Prince de Conti*, were commanded respectively by Captains Dufresne Marion and Beaulieu-Tréhouard.[93]

But even now, as Lochiel, Doctor Archie, Lochgarry and John Roy Stewart with, according to Chamber's history, over a hundred more men[94] were taken out by tender to the ships there was further delay. According to an eyewitness:

> About six in the evening, after sitting to supper, a message came from Le Conti, upon which Colonel Warren and the Captain of the Frigate got up in a great hurry, got on their best clothes, ordered us on board our Vessell with our chests where we remained guarded by their men and an officer until two next morning the 20th, when Colonel Warren and one of his officers came on board of us ..... he was in top spirits, telling us plainly that he had now got the Prince (meaning the young Pretender) on board with Lochiel ......

> and so they both sailed twixt two and three in the morning, the wind very fresh at north …….[95]

The sails filled quickly, waves breaking against their bows as the ships in convoy left the mouth of Loch nan Uamh to reach the open sea.

Chapter 30
REFUGEES IN FRANCE

As the ships drew away from Scotland the eyes of both Cameron brothers must have been on the shore fading into the distance beyond their wake. Foremost in their minds was acute anxiety as to what was happening to their wives and children. Doctor Archie, in particular, was thinking of Jean, left with young children with no form of support. He must have prayed that her mother would help her, living as she did close by. Fortunately for his peace of mind, he was not to know, until much later, how desperate were her circumstances at the time.

It was nearly a year later, on 25th August 1747, when Bishop Forbes visited Jean in the lodgings in Edinburgh where she was staying while waiting to join Archie in France. Horrified to hear what had happened, he noted down every detail of the dreadful story she told:

> That it was a common practice amongst the red-coats after Culloden battle, dispersed up and down the Highlands, to raise the bodies of man, woman, and child out of the graves for greed of the linen, or whatever was wrapped about them, and after they had taken that off them to leave the bodies above ground. She herself had two children that died at that time, and she was advised to bury them privately in some remote heathy brae, to prevent their being taken up again; but she could not think of burying them in any other place than where their forefathers were laid, and therefore she was obliged to bribe a sergeant to keep the fellows from digging up the bodies again.[96]

The Bishop further noted that, as Cumberland had issued orders that the Camerons be singled out for special punishment, *'She and her poor children behoved to take to the hills, no house being safe in the whole country about them'.*[97] Speaking with great bitterness, she then told him how she had expected to receive help from her husband's elder brother, John Cameron of Fassiefern, but that this had failed to materialize. *'My brother-in-law John never came to see me when I was leaving the Countrie, nor never was in the least assisting to me while I stayed thogh I sent to him'.*[98]

Had Doctor Archie been aware of what his wife and children were suffering, he might have risked staying in Scotland. As it was, believing that either Jean's relations in Sunart or his brother John at Fassifern would help them, he sailed with his brother Lochiel for the safety of France.

The voyage round the north coast of Ireland was uneventful, a rare happening in those days of sail. Prince Charles seized the chance of dictating some of his account of all that had happened during his Scottish campaign to Doctor Archie, who wrote it down meticulously in his clear and beautiful hand.

Ships of the British navy were searching for them now that Charles's escape was widely known. But mercifully a fog descended as they neared the coast of France. On 10th October, just three weeks after leaving Scotland, they landed in the little fishing port of Roscoff in Brittany on the north coast of France.

Those who had sailed with him from Scotland watched from the deck as Charles went ashore in the ship's boat, cheered by the crews of the *L'Heureux* and the *Prince de Conti,* while both ships fired a deafening twenty-one gun salute.

Once on French soil the Prince, together with some of the men who had sailed with him, went on to the nearby town of Morlaix. Soon after their arrival, the

Cameron brothers Donald and Archie, to their great joy, were reunited with their father.

John Cameron, Old Lochiel, now over eighty, so delighted to welcome his two sons to the country of his adoption, was spared at the moment of their meeting of the dreadful knowledge that his third son, Father Alexander, was dying on a prison ship in the Thames.

Alexander's suffering, since his capture by Captain John Fergussone in Morar in July, had been appalling. A brutal man by all accounts, Fergussone had a particular hatred for Roman Catholic priests. Alexander was held in almost unbelievable squalor in the hold of the *Furnace* as she sailed round the north of Scotland and down the east coast of Britain to the Thames.

A report by a medical officer, Mr Minshaw, employed by the Commissioners for the Wounded and sent to investigate a similar prison ship, the *Pamela,* is almost too terrible to comprehend. He wrote that:

> On my looking down into the hold where the prisoners then were, (I) was saluted with such an intolerable smell that it was like to overcome me, tho' I was provided with proper herbs and my nostrils stuffed therewith...the prisoners were called up one by one, such as were able to come, and on being asked told their names, in what regiment or corps they served, of what age they were and when born. The number of those who came on deck were 54, many of whom were very ill as appeared by their countenance and their snail creep pace in ascending the ladder, being only just able to crawl up. 18 who were left below were said to be utterly incapable of coming up on deck unless by the help of a string (sling) which was thought unnecessary as two of the most hardy of the guards went down into the hold...To hear *(their)* description of the uncleanliness of that place is surpassing

> imagination, and too nautious to describe, so that, together with malignant fever raging amongst them, and another odious distemper peculiar to Scotchmen, may terminate in a more dreadful disease.[99]

Father Alexander's friends in London begged Lord Albermarle (who had succeeded Cumberland in command of the army) to do something to help the brother of Lochiel who was enduring such terrible treatment in the *Furnace.* Albermarle sent a doctor to visit him who, appalled by what he found, reported most bluntly that Father Alexander would certainly die unless promptly released. Told this, Lord Albermarle sent a party to collect him, but Fergussone flatly refused to surrender his prisoner to anyone unless under the direct order of the Duke of Newcastle, then the Minister for War.

Jacobite sympathizers in London sent a bed, some clothing and other necessities to Father Alexander in the *Furnace* but Fergussone swore in fury that if they even tried to put them on board he would sink their boat. Mortified they returned to shore but, by the mercy of providence, at this point Captain Fergussone was given command of a new frigate, called the *Nightingale,* in which he sailed from the Thames.

Father Alexander, left in the Furnace, shouted with all his remaining strength for a priest to come to him. The captain of another prison ship, a man very different from Fergussone, told one of his own captives, Father John Farquharson, of the piteous cries. Father John was ferried over to the *Furnace* where whom should he find but his great friend Father Alexander.

The new captain having given his permission, Father Sandy, as he was affectionately known, was taken to Father John's ship where, as his biographer Monsignor Thomas Wynne has so movingly described:

> for the first time in months he was able to breathe in pure clean air untainted by the foul stench of the prison ship. It must have been more welcoming than anything he could have imagined. There he was in the bright sunlight, with the unfamiliar sounds of the city close by, and the sound of the seagulls. This new world was so beautiful and remote from the pit of degradation below.[100]

Father John nursed him tenderly but Alexander's wasted body, ravaged by starvation and disease, was beyond all human care. On 19th October 1746 he died in the arms of his friend. The way of his passing was some consolation to his family, when news of it finally reached them in France.

King Louis XV, as soon as he heard of Prince Charles' coming, ordered the Chateau of St Antoine, a luxuriously furnished mansion in the Faubourg Saint-Antoine in Paris, to be made ready for his occupation. From there, the Prince hastened to Fontainebleau where the King, presiding over the Council of State, interrupted the proceedings to receive him with a great show of joy and affection. Charles then wrote to him requesting a state visit at which he intended to put forward his request for an army with which to return to Scotland.

In the meanwhile, as he waited for an answer, he bought new clothes. He had reached France without a single spare shirt to his name, but now the French ladies vied with each other for fragments of the torn and peat stained rags, precious relics of the hero that to them had Charles become.

Likewise his companions, the men who now amounted to his small court, who after months of living rough in the Scottish mountains looked like beggars from the Paris streets, and who were now able to make themselves presentable through the largesse of the King of France.

Chapter 31
VERSAILLE

In January 1747 (according to the Gregorian calendar) some four months after arriving in France, Doctor Archie is mentioned as having returned to his former position of the Prince's *aide-de-camp*. Therefore, together with his brother Lochiel, he was one of the train of attendants who accompanied Prince Charles on his state visit to Louis XV. A procession of coaches set out from St Antoine on the road to Versaille. In the first sat Lord Ogilvie, Lord Elcho, Old Gordon of Glenbucket and the non-juring clergyman Mr George Kelly. In the second Prince Charles, Lord Lewis Gordon, son of the Marquis of Huntley, and John Cameron, the French King's master of the horse. Two pages, smartly dressed, leant against the boot while footmen, wearing Charles' livery, walked on either side. A third coach followed with, behind it and riding on horseback Donald, the 'Young Lochiel', as he was known, and it seems safe to believe, his brother Doctor Archibald Cameron.[101]

The people of Paris, used as they were to the opulence of their own country's court, nonetheless applauded the appearance of the young Scottish Prince. An eyewitness describing him wrote:

> His dress had in it somewhat of uncommon elegance. His coat was rose-coloured velvet embroidered with silver and lined with silver tissue, his waistcoat was a rich gold brocade, with a spangled fringe set on the scollops. The cockade on his hat and the buckles on his shoes were diamonds: the George which he wore at his bosom and the order of St Andrew which he wore also, tied by a piece of green ribbon to one of the buttons of his waistcoat, were prodigiously illustrated with large brilliants: in short he glittered all over like the star which they tell you appeared at his nativity.[102]

His retinue, even in new coats and breeches, must have appeared as dowdy as pigeons to a peacock to the watchers who saw them ride by. The only existing portrait of Doctor Archie, depicted it would seem in Scotland sometime before the '45, shows him wearing a brown coat and waistcoat offset by a white cravat and ruffles on the wrists of his shirt. If, in this instance, he was dressed in much the same way, the crowds would hardly have noticed him as, together with his brother and the younger members of the entourage, they rode behind the coaches which pulled by splendid horses and mounted by uniformed postillions, trundled over the streets of Paris on that late autumn day.

Reaching Versaille their eyes were dazzled both by the elegance of the façade, built in the baroque style on the order of Louis XIV, and by the water of the fountains sparkling in the low rays of the sun. The days they spent there were pleasurable. According to an anonymous writer the Prince *'supped with the King and the royal family and he and his followers were magnificently entertained'.* Doctor Archie, for one, would probably have relished a dish of porridge rather than the over-spiced dishes smothered in rich sauces on which the court dined every day. Also he may have struggled with conversation, being a poor linguist as his wife afterwards claimed.

During their visit Prince Charles was showered with compliments, but King Louis constantly evaded a direct answer to his request for an army to return to Scotland to renew the war which, if given this support, he felt certain he would win. The Prince, according to Young Glengarry, in a conversation with Bishop Forbes, had been obliged to give Lochiel full security for his estates before he would raise his clan. Consequently, under the present circumstances, all he could do was to try to secure a French regiment. He approached King Louis again and again without success, but eventually the French king did give Lochiel the command of the

French Albany regiment. In a letter to King James, Lochiel wrote:

> I told H.R.H. that Lord Ogilvie or others might incline to make a figure in France: but my ambition was to serve the Crown, and serve my country, or perish with itt. H.R.H. say'd he was doing all he could to return *(with forces to Scotland)* but persisted in his resolution to procure me a Regiment.
>
> If it is obtained, I shall accept it out of respect to the Prince, but I hope Yr. M. will approve of the resolution I have taken to share in the fate of the people I have undone, and if they must be sacrificed to die along with them. It is the only way I can free myself from the reproach of their blood, and shew the disinterested zeal with which I have lived and shall dye, your Majesty's most humble, most Obedient, and most humble subject and servant,
>
> Donald Cameron.[103]

In November The Prince moved into a rented apartment in L'Hotel d'Hollande, on the quay in Paris, where his brother Henry, the Duke of York, occupied another. Charles lived quietly, entertaining only members of his immediate suite, of whom Archie Cameron was one.[104]

King Louis, while prevaricating over the Prince's request, nonetheless made certain that the exiled Jacobites received grants of money, known as 'gratifications', from the French government. In a list, dated November 1746, 4,000 livres were awarded to Lochiel *'Chef de Camerons Brigadier et Colonel'.* Doctor Archie, *'Cameron Colonel',* given the rank of physician in his brother's regiment,[105] received 3,000 livres as did their octogenarian father *'Lochiel l'ainé commission de Colonel'.*[106] Another 1,000 livres was paid to Archibald Cameron in January 1747. *(twenty-four livres = one Louis d'or, a Louis being the equivalent of one English guinea)* Archie was later to write that, living as he did with the Prince in the Chateau de St Antoine, he had managed to save a considerable amount of his 'gratifications' to provide for his wife and family when, as he was hoping, they would be able to leave Scotland to join him in France.

News from home came seldom, nearly always it was bad. His wife and children had been forced to go into hiding. Not only had two of his children died but another daughter had been stripped of all her clothes by Government troops.[107]

Whether the girl was physically assaulted is not revealed. It may have been thought indecent to mention it for fear of besmirching the reputation of a young lady of high social standing, related as she was to Lochiel.

Horrifying in its barely believable savagery as this tale appears to be, it is certainly comparable to that of Jean Cameron's sister, wife of Cameron of Glennevis, who was found by soldiers hiding in a cave. One of the men noticed that she was concealing something bulky, which he took to be of value, beneath her plaid. Noticing a silver brooch holding the plaid to her shoulder, he seized it with one hand while slicing through the material with the point of his sword. A piercing cry sent him reeling back in shock as the plaid fell away to reveal a young child, his throat injured by the sword. The little boy recovered, but for the rest of his life bore the scar of the soldier's wound.

On 16th October 1746, Prince Charles wrote to his father from Paris to tell him of the Cameron brothers' postings. His father, then in Albano, replied almost immediately on 7th November, telling his dearest Carluccio how happy he was that Lochiel had at last got a regiment:

> I remark, and take well of you, that you do not directly ask of me to declare Lochiel's

title......Lochiel's interest and reputation in his own country, and his being at the head of a regiment in France, will make him more considered than any empty title I could give him; and as he knows the justice both you and I do to his merit and services, I am sure he is too reasonable to take amiss my not doing now what would be of no use to him, and would be very improper and inconvenient to us.[108]

Chapter 32
BEYOND THE PYRENEES

By the end of the year 1746, after three months in France, Prince Charles had begun to understand that his hopes of persuading King Louis to give him an army to take to Scotland were unlikely to be realized. Peace was on the agenda. Negotiations to end the War of the Austrian Succession after five years of fighting between France and Britain, supporting rival claimants, were taking place. Soon, as now seemed inevitable, King Louis would no longer need the diversion of a Scottish rebellion to draw Cumberland away from Flanders.

Dispirited, but resilient against accepting the loss of all his hopes, Charles decided to try to enlist the help of Scotland's other erstwhile ally, King Ferdinand VI of Spain.

Without permission from King Louis, in a total breach of protocol involving secrecy, he left the French king's domains to ride south to the papal enclave of Avignon. With him went Doctor Archie, acting again as his *aide-de-camp*, as well as one other attendant, most probably a groom. Reaching Avignon, Archie must have written to his brother to tell him of their safe arrival. In Paris Lochiel received the news with dismay and on 23rd February 1747 he wrote an impassioned letter to the Prince:

> I am very glad to hear that your journey has proved agreeable, and that you are safely arrived at Avignon. Though your going thither was, and still is, a matter of the greatest affliction to all your true friends, and me in particular; yet upon considering that step in every shape, I persuade myself that your Royal Highness may give it such turn, and make such of it, as will not only make your apology to the King of France, but in the end effectually confute the disadvantageous

opinion that the world has conceived of it, and force the public to admire your Royal Highness' abilities in the cabinet, as well as your courage and heroism in the field...I must beg your Royal Highness will be pleased to observe, that, since you left this place, the talk and expectation of peace is become more general and popular. It is said the Marshal de Belleisle, who is quickly expected here, will be sent as Plenipotentiary to the conference of Breda, and from thence into England; so that though the King's equipages are getting ready for the field, few people make any doubt but a peace will soon be concluded; and I remark such are the universal desires of it in this country, that there is reason to fear the Elector of Hanover and his allies will obtain any terms they please to ask in relation to your Royal Highness, which the Court of France will think they can grant with a good grace since Your Royal Highness has, of your own accord, left their dominions...

As for the disposition of Scotland, if we could return to the Highlands with artillery, arms, and ammunition, and only four or five dispositions of foot, we would not only relieve our distressed friends and save the remains of the country, but deliver the whole kingdom of Scotland from the slavery to which it is, or soon will be, reduced...Indeed I hear from all hands, and have great reason to believe, that all Scotsmen, not excepting those who are most distinguished in the Government's service, are so incensed at the inhumanity with which the Elector has proceeded, and the neglect they have met with since the unhappy action of Culloden, that they only want an opportunity to show their resentment.

For heaven's sake, sir, be pleased to consider these circumstances with the attention their importance deserves, and that your honour, your essential interest, the preservation of the

Royal cause, and the bleeding state of your suffering friends require of you.[109]

Lochiel begged the Prince to *'write a proper letter with his own hand',* to the King of France, to explain that he had only gone to Avignon to avoid suspicion of the present government, because he knew that it was impossible for the French navy to transport even a small body of troops into Britain, unless in the utmost secrecy. He then suggested that he should send the bearer, most probably O'Sullivan, to tell the King *'what he judged necessary for a renewed rising in Scotland'.* He himself believed that if only a small body of French troops could gain a foothold on the west coast, King Louis would then reinforce them *'with your brave Irish regiments'*. He would also send three or four thousand men into Wales, and his English supporters would rise as soon as he was master of the field in Scotland.[110]

By the time Lochiel's letter reached Avignon, Prince Charles and Doctor Archie had already set out for Spain. In the freezing weather of late February, they most likely took the route to Pau. Riding together, almost knee to knee, Charles talked ceaselessly of his hopes and ambitions, making it plain to the doctor that his hopes of leading another expedition to Scotland were still uppermost in his mind.

As the road climbed into the mountains their conversation dwindled as both they and their horses struggled forward, heads down against a cruel wind. The men with their mouths muffled could only shout a few words as, keeping a tight rein to stop their horses from stumbling, they rode in the steps of Roland across the Pass of Roncesvalles into Spain.

Once in that country they found the travelling easier. The roads were largely straight and well built. Also there were post houses at regular intervals from which fresh horses could be hired. Despite the easier travelling, however, it was still a hard and tortuous journey for men, even used to rough living under harsh weather conditions as were they. Struggling on over ice bound roads through snow and rain, and winds so cold that they stung with the force of a knife, they at last rode wearily into the town of San Lorenzo de el Escorial, about twenty miles to the north-west of Madrid.

The Palace of San Lorenzo de el Escorial, combined with a royal monastery standing within high stone walls above a moat crossed by a bridge, had been built nearly two hundred years earlier, in 1559, by Philip II king of Spain. On the advice of his viceroy in Naples, he had engaged the man who became his royal architect, Juan Bautista de Toledo, already renowned for his work on the basilica of St Peter's in Rome. Together they had planned and constructed the magnificent edifice as the Christian centre of Spain.

The Royal Palace in Madrid having been destroyed by fire, was now in the process of being rebuilt. Therefore it was to the Royal Monastery, then the temporary residence of the bibliophile King Ferdinand VI and his wife, the plain but sensible Barbara Infanta of Portugal on whom he depended for advice, that Charles was conducted for an audience.

As in France all outward civility was shown. But Ferdinand, known as 'the learned', was determined under no circumstances to become involved in any form of conflict between France and England. Politely, but firmly, he refused to even countenance the idea of sending an army to Scotland to restore the Stuarts to the British throne.

José de Carvajal y Lancáster, Ferdinand's recently appointed First Secretary of State, an almost impossibly good looking man, magnificent in a gold embroidered waistcoat, lace ruffles on the wrists of his velvet coat, a gold chain of office round his neck, received him with much flattery, but gave no hint of any aid.

Frustrated and furious at the absolute refusals of both the King and his minister, however covertly disguised, Charles wrote to his father *'I thought there was not such fools as the French court, but I find it here far beyond it'.*[111]

It would seem that Ferdinand, however, as a consolation for the obvious disappointment he had caused, did give a sop to Prince Charles by agreeing to his special request that Doctor Archie Cameron be given a colonelcy in the Spanish army.

This was done on the assumption that ships with flour, brandy, soap and tobacco would be sent to the Highlands of Scotland and that Cameron should go with them, helping the distribution of this relief. So Doctor Archie remained in Spain until May 1747 when, realizing that the promised voyage to Scotland had been indefinitely postponed, he returned to his regiment in France.

With the prospect of the salary of a Spanish colonel added to that of a captaincy in the Albany Regiment, his finances at last seemed secure enough for his family to join him but, in fact, the Spanish salary never materialized.

Chapter 33
REUNION

Lochiel's wife Anne had already sailed from Scotland to join her husband, and now Archie wrote to Jean in August urging her to make the move, but she could not travel immediately due, it would seem, to commitments at home. On 25th August 1747, when Bishop Forbes visited Jean in her lodgings in Edinburgh, he heard the appalling tale of all that she had suffered at the hands of the Government soldiers. Furthermore she told him that she had written to her husband accusing him of failing to keep in touch:

> I am hear at a time that I never heard from you ever since you went to Holand and did not know whether you was dead or alaiv, nor even if you was in life, whither you was in condition to mintean me or my children.[112]

He may not have got the letter being at that time in Spain. In it she gave him an explanation of what was happening to the children who had survived. The boys, John, Donald, Allan, Duncan and Charles, and the girls, Bel (Isobel) and Peggy. She told him that:

> 'On my way hear I left Dunkie at Achmor *(home of their cousin MacGregor Drummond of Balhaldie)* wher he wil be wel taken care of and Alan with an onest old farmer at Dunblean *(Dunblane)* wher heal be very hapie.' *Donald had been left in the care of the knight beside Stirling* 'wher he would fare no worse than the rest but I have sent for him hear this day in order to carie him along with me according to your desair, little Pegie is staying with your agent in this place who have no children of his own and he and his ladie as discret a cuple as ever I new. Johnie and Bel are now with me and your Bel is weaker than ever you sau hir so that her condition makes me and hirself verie unhapie'.[113]

Lord Amulree says that Jean arrived in Flanders with only two of her surviving children, but this may be a mistake. It is thought that Bel, whose frail health was a cause of so much concern, died in France before 1753.

Jean Cameron's journey was not without incident. Reaching Breda, in the Netherlands, she was interviewed in her lodgings by an English officer, on the instructions of Lord Albermarle. The officer's written report states:

> I found her with a girl she call'd her daughter, a boy of about nine years old, a man and maid servant, her eldest son a lad of about 14 being gone out, but where she would not say.[114]

.

A document in the Forfeited Estates papers in Register House, Edinburgh, proves this to be John:

> To the Right Honourable the Lords of Council and Session. The claim of Mrs Jean Cameron, spouse to Arch. Cameron Chyrurgeon in Strontian and John Cameron their eldest son.[115]

Held in custody until the following 5th February, Jean was at last set free, but whether she then joined Archie in France or, in the unsettled political situation, stayed in the lodgings in Breda, remains unknown. Wherever and whenever it happened their reunion must have been joyful even if prevailing uncertainty threatened to again tear them apart. On 24th April, three months after Jean's arrival, a conference was held at Aix-la-Chapelle to arrange the terms of peace. The summer passed before, on 18th October 1748, a treaty was s+igned which finally brought the War of the Austrian Succession to a close. The terms included the ultimatum that Prince Charles must leave France. Warned of the danger, he nonetheless went to the opera where he was arrested. Tied with silk cords he was taken to the Chateau de Vincennes before being deported into Papal territory at Avignon.

His immediate household, of about thirty people, was then removed for a short time to the Bastille, the fortress known formally as the Bastille Sainte-Antoine. The state prison of the kings of France, it harboured a sinister atmosphere, as if prescient of the misery and bloodshed that the yet unborn dauphin and his family would endure. In the case of Prince Charles' servants, held as they were as state prisoners, their treatment appears to have been lenient. Among the archives of the fortress is a letter to Doctor Archie from his uncle, Ludovic Cameron of Torcastle, (eighth son of Sir Euan) dated 15th December, asking him to collect three shirts and one nightcap for him from the washerwoman and to pay her for her work.[116]

How Jean and the children survived during his imprisonment is a mystery. But a letter proves that, once released from the Bastille, although unable to communicate with Prince Charles, Archie wrote to King James in Rome, asking for his help in extracting the promised colonel's salary from Spain. The King did appeal to Cardinal Joaquín Fernández de Portocarrero Mendoza, the Spanish ambassador to the Papal States, but without any success.

Meanwhile, although there was no sign of the Spanish money, Archie's 'gratification' from the French King did continue to be paid. But for how long no one could tell.

The Treaty of Aix-la-Chapelle can only be described as a death blow to the Jacobite cause. All plans for an invasion of Scotland were now cancelled, the Marquis de Puysieux, Louis' Foreign Minister, declaring that Lochiel was *'sunk in an extremity of grief and despair'*. In the autumn of 1748, just before the treaty was signed, the leading Scottish exiles met in Paris to discuss the desperate situation in which they now found themselves. They agreed that under no circumstances must the Prince be allowed to lose all connection with King Louis. Lochiel himself must bluntly tell him so, it being known that in his present state of mind he was unlikely to listen to anyone else.

Instead of hastening to Avignon to use his influence with Prince Charles, Lochiel, perhaps already feeling ill, returned to his regiment at Bergues, in Flanders. It was there, on 26th October, just eight days after the Treaty of Aix-la-Chapelle was signed, that he was seized by the sudden illness which killed him at the age of forty-eight.

On 4th November 1748, his cousin, MacGregor Drummond of Balhaldie, wrote to King James in Rome:

> it becomes cruel in me now to be obliged to begin to inform you of the loss your Majesty has of the most faithful and zealously devoted subject ever served any Prince, in the person of Donald Cameron of Lochiel. He died the 26 of last month of an inflammation within his head at Borgue *(Bergues)* where he had been for some time with his regiment, and where I had the melancholy satisfaction to see all means used for his preservation, but to no valuable effect.[117]

Balhaldie's description of Donald's illness suggests a brain tumour or possibly a stroke. To those who knew him he died of a broken heart.

Donald had been XIXth chief of Clan Cameron for only a year after his father, living like his grandfather to a good old age, had expired at the age of eighty-two.

Inheriting the yoke of responsibility both for his family and his clan when only nineteen, Donald had been a father figure to his siblings in their youth. Now it was his brother Archie, whose lack of attention to his studies had once caused Donald much anxiety, who took over the supervision of his brother's sixteen year old son, twentieth chief of the Camerons of Lochiel.

Chapter 34
RIVALS FOR COMMAND

In January 1746, Alasdair Ruadh MacDonell, Young Glengarry, when held in the Tower of London, wrote to Waters the banker in Paris asking for money. This coincided with the tragedy of the death of his brother Aeneas, so unfortunately shot by a man of Clanranald's regiment at Falkirk.

Money was sent to the Tower which Young Glengarry used to buy food, not only for himself, but for other unfortunate prisoners who might otherwise have died of starvation, this being one of the few acts of generosity ever recorded to his name. Released in July 1747, he was hanging around Paris looking hopefully for some form of employment.

He thought that his moment had come when Lochiel died leaving a vacancy for the Albany regiment's command. Young Glengarry tried at once to get the colonelcy but, on the orders of King Louis it was given instead to Lochiel's son. His uncle Doctor Archie, in *locum tenens*, wrote from Paris to King James on 16th December 1748:

> I, upon having the honour, for the first time of troubling your Majesty with a letter, or rather an apology for not writing sooner, to acquaint your Majesty that my brother Lochiel died on the 26th of October, last of ten days' sickness, at a time most fatal and unlucky for his family and his clan it could have happened, having just completed his regiment at great expense and considerable exertions, and upon the way of reaping the benefits of it towards the maintaining of his wife and six children, and providing for some of his friends and dependents, who lost comfortable living to join him in the late desperate and unsuccessful struggle we had in behalf of his Royal Highness in Scotland, and for a little time

> in England; but now, by his death they are reduced to the miserable situation they were in before the King of France was pleased, through the application of his Royal Highness, to grant the regiment. Next day, after my brother's death, I brought my nephew, of sixteen years of age, in order to lay him flat at his Majesty's feet; then by His Highness' approbation, to present him to the King of France. Accordingly his Highness made application, and on the 7th of November gave in a memorial asking the regiment for my nephew, and if thought too young, that I, being at present captain of Grenadiers, commandant (in absence of the lieutenant-colonel) and his uncle, would manage the regiment till he was of age, as I am resolved to attend and serve my brother's children and my own, especially as that of Spain does not answer... All our corps, and the remains of Lochiel's family are unanimously inclined to have my nephew, and regiment if obtained, under my directions at present, as is my nephew himself. I beg your Majesty will give assistance towards it. [118]

On 23rd of the same month Doctor Cameron wrote again to the exiled king, repeating his requests of the previous letter before, on 23rd February, young John Cameron wrote himself:

> I have appointed Archibald, my uncle, curator and sole manager in all my affairs. I beg leave to inform your Majesty the motives that induced me to this step, which are: he is my full uncle, so that I believe his sincerity to be unexceptionable...if during my minority, they should be commanded by him; to this step I have the unanimous consent of all my friends from Scotland, by express, upon hearing of my father's death, and the officers of his regiment. [119]

On 14th January 1749, King James replied from Rome. Acknowledging both letters he wrote:

> It is true I took a very particular share in the great loss you have lately made. Being well acquainted with your brothers, and your family's merit with me, and truly sensible of the many marks they have given us of it, as I am now of the sentiments expressed in your letters. By what I lately heard I am afraid Lochiel's regiment will be reformed, but in that case I understand that the officers will be taken care of and your nephew and his mother have pensions. I should be very sorry for this reform, neither do I see what I can well do to prevent it, after the very strong recommendation I had already made that the said regiment might be given to your nephew; but you may be sure that nothing that can depend upon me will ever be neglected that will tend to be of the advantage to your family, and of so many brave and honest gentlemen. This would be a very improper time to mention you to the Court of Spain, but some months hence I shall be able to recommend you to that Court, and in such a manner as I hope may succeed, if they are in any wise disposed to favour you. The Duke *(of York, Prince Charles's brother)* takes very kindly of you the compliments you make him, and I have often heard him speak of you with much esteem and in the manner you deserve. I don't write in particular to your nephew, since I could but repeat what I have here said, and to which I have nothing to add, but to assure you both of my constant regard and kindness.[120]

Young John Cameron did get his regiment, as is shown by another letter from Doctor Archie to King James, dated Paris 23rd December 1748:

> Upon my laying my nephew at his Royal Highness's feet, his Highness was so good as to recommend to the Minister of War, Comte D'Argenson, the giving the regiment to my nephew, in lieu of his family's sufferings, upon which I, by the advice of general officers of the army, and at the unanimous desire of all the captains of the Albany regiment, I gave a memoir to the minister, asking the regiment for my nephew; but if thought too young to command it, I would take charge of it in his name during his minority, as his uncle, captain of grenadiers, and commander of the regiment of Albany, now upon the peace being concluded, I would undertake to recruit the regiment of our numerous, though much reduced clan, and other Scotch we have interest with.[121]

Doctor Archie continues to remind the king of his brother's *'suffering upon the misgiving of the late attempt in Scotland'* and of his own share in it:

> and of my having a wife and throng family of children to maintain. I plainly understand they *(the French government)* have compassion for us, which will give my nephew a better chance for the regiment...of which I was advised this day by a letter from my wife, from Graveline's being told so by Major Ogilvie of our regiment, as also by our cousin, Balhaldy.

The mention of his wife is the real point of this letter. He explained that:

> he was sorry to be obliged to trouble your Majesty in recommending the maintenance of me, my wife, and family to this court...having got no pay, nor no appearance of it as yet, from the court of Spain; and the reason I was not named lieutenant-colonel of my brother's regiment, as

> his Highness and my brother intended long before the regiment was granted, it was thought my pay in Spain would punctually answer, though I even all that time had not absolute faith in its being paid duly, which my family would require.[122]

He continues to affirm that he would not resent the regiment being given to Cluny MacPherson, as had apparently been an option, he being *'a worthy, honest and brave man, who suffered all the common misfortunes'*, but nonetheless maintained that he had *'the best title to expect it, especially as my nephew puts his whole confidence in me, in relation to the management of his affairs during his minority'*.

The upshot of all this correspondence was that command of the Albany regiment was conferred upon young John.

Chapter 35
THE JACOBITE JUDAS

Not everyone was pleased. To Young Glengarry the news of the appointment came like a blow between the eyes. Already highly resentful, both of his own imprisonment and that of his father in Edinburgh Castle, as well as the accidental death of his brother Aeneas, he took the appointment of John Cameron to the command of the Albany Regiment as an insult aimed directly at himself. Enraged he wrote to King James, telling him of his poverty resulting from the recent rebellion and of his own suitability to command the regiment on account of both experience and age.

The King replied through his secretary, James Edgar, that he was unable to interfere and assist Glengarry, as he had already recommended young Lochiel. He then continued to say that *'His Majesty is sorry to find you so low in your circumstances and reduced to such straits at present as you mention',* but explained that he could not help him being much impoverished himself. Then, in what he hoped would be some consolation, he sent him a duplicate of his grandfather's warrant to be a Peer. *'You will see that it is signed by H.M. and I can assure you that it is an exact duplicate copie out of the book of entrys of such like papers'.*[123]

Thwarted and driven to exasperation by what can only be described as the ridiculous gift of a document proving a peerage to a virtually starving man Glengarry, still in Paris in the summer of 1749, wrote, on 9th June, to Prince Charles's brother, the Cardinal Duke of York. To him he explained that while in the Tower, the Court of France had sent him *'unlimited credit'* as a Highland chief. But now the French War Office were demanding repayment of the advance, and had detained four years of his pay in the French service. He could not receive money from home, his father being in prison, and his lands entirely destroyed. Such was his tragic tale.

Glengarry was certainly penniless when, by some means or other, he reached London in August of the same year. Desperate for money, he sold his sword and shoe buckles, the only things of value he possessed. To help him a priest, Father Leslie, who had befriended him in Paris, pledged a gold repeater to Clanranald. The watch actually belonged to Mrs Murray, still at that time with her husband, who was furious when told of Father Leslie's blatant robbery.

Alasdair Ruadh, short tempered as his hair was red, attributed the loss of the much vaunted military appointment to Archie Cameron, believing him to have influenced King Louis into giving it to his nephew instead of himself. Resentment, fired by his state of penury, seems to have unhinged his mind.

On a day in late August 1749, Sir Duncan Campbell of Lochnell, the member for Argyllshire, was leaving the House of Commons when he heard someone calling his name. Turning, he recognized the slim figure, prematurely bent by illness, as none other than the Secretary of State, Mr Henry Pelham, himself.

Drawing him aside Pelham, in a quiet voice, asked him if he knew Glengarry? Sir Duncan, somewhat bewildered, replied that he did know the old man but not the young. Pelham then told him it was Young Glengarry that he spoke of:

> for that he came to him offering his most faithful and loyal services to the Government in any shape they thought proper, as he came from feeling the folly of any further concern with the ungrateful family of Stuart, to whom he and his family had been too long attached, to the absolute ruin of themselves and country.[124]

It would be nice to know what Pelham, then *de facto* Prime Minister, made of this tall, red-haired Scot, who presented himself at his residence, number eleven Downing Street, the house bequeathed to the Treasurer by his predecessor Walpole on whose shoulders he had risen to power.

Pelham, as a man of the world, must have taken in at first glance the threadbare condition of his visitor's clothes, the gaunt frame and the pallor, so evident of the poor diet on which, by his general appearance, he must have existed for some time. If doubtful, or indeed contemptuous initially of his exterior, he soon began to realize, as he spoke to him, that what he had to offer was nonetheless beyond value. Only three years after its suppression, renewed rebellion in the Highlands was an ever present threat to the country's stability. This man, it soon became evident, was not only the son of a clan chief of importance, but as such was at the heart of the network of Jacobite agents in Scotland.

Pelham, or someone else of influence, must have given him money, thereby enlisting him as an agent, to be paid for the secrets he revealed. Glengarry was starving in August, but by December, on the word of Aeneas MacDonald the banker who, taken prisoner was tried in London, he had '*plenty of cash*'.[125]

Did his sudden affluence spring from the coffers of the Treasury, or was there another reason why Glengarry, so obviously destitute in the autumn of 1749, should suddenly appear affluent in the space of a mere four months? The question remains an enigma like much of Glengarry's life.

Chapter 36
SCOTLAND

Following the death of his brother Lochiel, and the appointment of his nephew to the colonelcy of the Albany regiment, Doctor Archie Cameron, for reasons unstated, transferred from the Albany Regiment to Lord Ogilvie's Regiment.

Raised in France by David, Lord Ogilvie, eldest son of the Earl of Airlie, in 1747, the regiment was amalgamated with the French army *'where the officers were treated like gentlemen'*. Initially Doctor Archie, with the rank of captain, moved with the regiment to Lille, the medieval capital of Flanders, captured from the Dutch by Louis XIV in 1666, since when, following the first Treaty of Aix la Chapelle, it had been part of France. Here he was stationed for a period of about two years. No longer a medical officer, he seems to have acted as adjutant during the time he was there.

Amongst the Scots Papers in the Record Office in Edinburgh is a mysterious letter from an anonymous writer, clearly a Latin scholar, which gives a fair idea of the animosity that was festering in Scotland between Cluny MacPherson and MacDonell of Glengarry and the Camerons of Glennevis over the gold sent to Prince Charles from France. Dated 26th January 1748, the unknown person, using classical names as a code, sent a warning to someone of influence, it would seem in government office:

> Scyphax *(Cluny)* is still in the country and there are disturbances between him and the Dorians *(Camerons)* and Aetolians *(Glengarrys)* over the goods left by the Young Mogul *(Prince Charles)* Nothing but stealing and plundering prevails in all quarters here.[126]

Evidently, it was in an attempt to settle what sounded like a dangerous dispute that Archie Cameron travelled to Scotland in September 1749. Specifically he made the journey on the instruction of King James, to consult with Cluny MacPherson on the dispersal of the Loch Arkaig gold.[127]

With him, according to another account, went Major Kennedy, one of the two or three other men with whom Archie had dug so carelessly, leaving footprints behind them in the mud, on that dark night, now four years past.

Significantly, at much the same time, Young Glengarry went to Scotland with his cousin, Donald MacDonald of Lochgarry, referred to by almost all sources as a truly loyal man where, so it is claimed, Glengarry helped himself to some of the gold. As reported by Lord Crawford (making much use of capital letters):

> He *(Glennevis)* does not deny but that his brother Angus, Lochgary, Young Glengarry, Angus McIan and he went into Badenoch in the winter of 1749, after the troops were gone from thence, with a view to meeting Clunie, but that while Lochgary, and Young Glengarry had their Interview at a shieling opposite to Dalwhinnie, he was desired by Clunie to keep at the House of Dalwhinnie till sent for, and that neither Angus nor he coud be allowed to speak with him, tho' he sent repeated messages by Clunie's Piper, and a young brother of Clunie's. That he lay in the same room with Young Glengarry at Dalwhinnie, and early in the morning, the young brother of Clunie brought Glengarry a Bag which might contain two or three Hundred guineas, and counted them out to him, and that he understood Glengarry got, in the whole, by that expedition about Two Thousand (this includes the money got by Glengarry in Edinburgh, out of Murray's original 5,000 louis, entrusted to his

> brother-in-law Mr MacDougal). He farther says that the money remitted abroad by Clunie was carried away by his Brother-in-Law McPherson of Brechachie to Major Kennedy in the North of England.[128]

Glennevis who, having been held prisoner in Fort William had just been admitted to bail, blamed Young Glengarry with great bitterness for his arrest. He also told Lord Crawford that Young Glengarry had forged King James's name.

How much Young Glengarry, *'had it in'* for Doctor Archie, believing him to have been instrumental in robbing him of what he took to be his rightful command of Albany's Regiment, becomes obvious in the letter he wrote on 16th January 1750, (this date is according to the Gregorian Calendar which was only adopted in Scotland in September 1752) to James Edgar from Boulogne-sur-mer. Referring to his recent visit to Scotland he said:

> it is with regret I find myself obliged to acquaint you, in order that you inform his Majesty, of the conduct of Doctor Archibald Cameron, brother to the late Lochiel, whose behaviour, when lately in the Highlands, has greatly hurt his Majesty's interest by acquainting all he conversed with that now they must shift for themselves, for his Majesty and Royal Highness had given up all thoughts of ever being restored. I have prevented the bad consequences that might ensue from such notions; but one thing I could not prevent, was his taking 6000 Louis-d'ors of the money left in the country by his Royal Highness, which he did without any opposition, as he was privy to where the money was laid, only Cluny MacPherson obliged him to give a receipt for it...I am credibly informed that he designs to lay this money in the hands of a merchant at Dunkirk, and enter partners with

> him... and he hopes that James will detain Archibald Cameron in Rome, till his own arrival. He protests that it is *'very disagreeable to him'* to give this information.[129]

The man's effrontery in telling lies so damaging to Archie is almost unbelievable, as indeed it was to King James. Having read Archie's meticulously produced *Memorial Concerning the Loch Arkaig Treasure*,(see Appendix page 212) he particularly noticed the last paragraph, in which Glengarry wrote that *'Clunie's brother-in-law told* (Cameron of) *Fassiefern that Glengarry, throw the faith of his credential got 300 Louis from Clunie, and six hundred Louis from Angus Cameron, Clunie's trustee.'*

Prince Charles also received a letter from Glengarry, in which he said:

> as to the account I sent of the embezzling of the money by Clunie and Dr Cameron, with some others of his family, most of the money is still in the country...people have spread a report that I touched considerably of it when last in Scotland, I hope your Royal Highness will approve of the trifle I or any of my friends received.[130]

James, immediately suspicious, wrote at once to his son. Dating his letter 17th March 1750, the King pointed out to Charles that someone, he obviously suspected Glengarry, had tried to obtain money by forging his signature:

> You will remark that at the end of Archy's paper, it is mentioned as if a certain person should have made use of my name in S____d, and have even produced a letter supposed to be mine to prove that he was acting by commission from me: what there may be in the bottom of this I know not, but I think it necessary you should know that since your return from S____d I never either

> employed or authorized the person, or anybody else, to carry any commissions on politick affairs to any of the three kingdoms.[131]

Glengarry had indeed forged the King's signature. Aeneas MacDonald, in a letter dated 12th October 1751, writes that he has heard a report '*too audacious to be believed; that Glengarry had counterfeited his Majesty's signature to gett the money that he gott in Scotland'.*

Yet Glengarry, unaware that he had been rumbled, had now become a double agent. While continuing to write to both King James and his son assuring them of his loyalty, he was living, presumably at the expense of the British government, in Beaufort Buildings in the Strand.

Handsome as he was, he was enjoying the life of a well-heeled young man about town. He was planning to marry a lady of good family, or so at least he professed but perhaps, like his other manifestations, this was all part of a charade.

Glennevis, held prisoner in Fort William, persisted in his resentment against Young Glengarry, believing him to have betrayed both himself and his brother Angus for having helped themselves to some of the gold buried near Loch Arkaig in 1749. He also accused him of forging King James's name.

Chapter 37
THE CURSE OF THE GOLD

Detailed accounts, by both Doctor Archie and Cluny MacPherson, prove how the money was spent. (see Appendix II, page 212)

That it was Glengarry who accused Archie of the theft of money, which he himself had acquired by forging the King's signature, seems established beyond any reasonable doubt. Horrified on hearing that, thanks to an informer, (whose identity was then probably unknown) he was being accused of theft, Archie immediately left for Rome, determined to clear himself before the King.

His wife, on failing to hear from him, thought he might have got lost in Marseilles. She contacted the Jacobites there, asking them to keep an eye open for him, telling them that *'they would quickly know him as a foreigner by his not speaking the language'* although by then he had been in France for three years!

He did reach Rome eventually, probably travelling by sea from Marseilles through the Mediterranean, this being the easiest and most common form of transport at the time and, once in the Eternal City, he made his way to the Palazzo Muti.

The large town house in the Piazza dei Santi Apostoli was owned by the Muti Papazzurris, one of Rome's patrician families, for whom it was designed in the Baroque style by the architect Mattia de Rossi in 1644. Since 1719, the Popes Clement XI and Innocent XIII had rented the whole complex of residences, of which it was part, for James Edward Stuart and his family, rightful heirs to the throne of Great Britain as they believed them to be. A building of four floors with the main entrance leading to an inner courtyard, the grandeur was enhanced by classical statues on the roof surmounting a balustrade.

Archie, on his arrival, would have been escorted through the inner courtyard to the main entrance door on the first floor. From there, following a liveried and bewigged footman, he would have climbed the staircase to one of the high ceilinged reception rooms on the first floor. There King James would have received him as the loyal compatriot who, despite Glengarry's allegations against him, he still knew him to be.

That Archie did bring some of the gold from Scotland is shown by a letter from his uncle Ludovic Cameron of Torcastle to Prince Charles (dated 21st November 1753) in which he said that Archie had told him about it in Rome *'where I happened to be at the time'.* Anxious to clear himself of any accusation that he had taken some for himself, Torcastle assured the Prince that *'I never touched one farthing of it, or ever will'.*[132]

Glengarry, who is also known to have been in Rome in that spring of 1750, entered the Palazzo in a very different way. Coming at night he found his way to the cellar from which a secret stair led to the rooms above. King James did receive him but treated his information, particularly his rather ridiculous insistence on Cameron's supposed theft of the buried gold, with great suspicion.

It was probably in Rome that Archie contracted the illness that subsequently affected his health, and which sounds so like the malaria spread by mosquitoes from the swamps close to the city. Returning to Lille, where Lord Ogilvie's regiment was stationed, he was ill with what he described as *'a most dangerous fever and ague which confined him all the winter wholly to his room and mostly to his bed, which has shattered his constitution much ever since'.*[133]

At that time he noted that two of his children were still being taken care of by friends or relations in Scotland. Then, in the following year of 1751, another child was born, *'who had the honour of being called James after the King'.*[134] This leads to the speculation that one of his elder sons had already been named Charles, an idea based on Archie's close association with the Prince. It has further been suggested that this boy grew up to become the noted architect, Charles Cameron, designer of the Catherine Palace near St Petersburg, for Catherine the Great. This, however, is unlikely, the man in question being, almost certainly, the son of a joiner in London.

It would seem that because of Archie's illness it was Jean, his intrepid wife who, leaving the children with him, went to Edinburgh in the autumn of the year in which her last baby, little James, was born. Arriving in the city in the month of October, she was arrested and interrogated by Charles Erskine of Tinwald, the Lord Justice Clerk, senior judge in the Court of Session, then acting as a political agent of the Crown. Her belongings searched and nothing treasonable found, he accepted her word that she had come over to see friends and relatives *'on matters relating only to the squabbles at their sham court who the persons were who had secreted the money, each of them putting it upon the other'.*

She returned to Lille to find her husband recovered at last from his illness, but still suffering pain from the bullet which, since Falkirk, had remained embedded in his chest.

Chapter 38
BETRAYAL

Tobias Smollett's novel 'Peregrine Pickle' was published in 1751. Glengarry, said to have greatly admired it, is believed to have taken his pseudonym 'Pickle' as the code name under which he henceforth corresponded with Pelham, from the title of the book.

Andrew Lang (1844–1912) wrote two books identifying Young Glengarry with Pickle, notably by his spelling of the word 'who' as 'how'. Moreover his intimate knowledge both of people and places shown in his correspondence makes him the prime suspect as revealed by Lang's studious research.

While it is hard to disregard this, it must be remembered that Glengarry was far from being the only Highlander totally ruined by the Stuarts. Much as his father, King James III & VIII, had done before him, 'Bonny Prince Charlie', romantic adventurer that he was, left families bankrupt and homeless, their houses and castles in many cases burnt to the ground. Most grievous of all was the knowledge that, while the Stuarts were living in comfort in Rome, those who had risked everything for them in Scotland were left without any hope of compensation and barely a word of thanks.

That Glengarry was by now suspected of treachery is shown by an anonymous letter, forwarded by John Holker a Jacobite who, taken prisoner at Carlisle, had been held in the infamous Newgate prison from which he managed to escape. By then one of the leaders of espionage in Europe, he had somehow come across the information which he sent on to young Waters, the banker, in Paris: a copy going to James Edgar in Rome.

Already, on 30th November 1751, someone sealing his letter with the signet of a stag's head gorged, and a stag under a tree in the shield, had written to Waters informing him that Glengarry's friend

Father Leslie (the seller of Mrs Murray's gold repeater) was untrustworthy, *'to my private knowledge an arrant rogue'.* Known to have been in London, he was now travelling to Lorraine specifically to spy on Prince Charles who was thought to have crossed the border from Italy into France illegally more than once.

More importantly, as far as Archie was concerned, the anonymous writer of a second letter, forwarded to Waters by John Holker, revealed that a regular correspondence existed between John Murray of Broughton, a traitor since turning King's evidence, and Samuel Cameron of Glennevis who, as a relation of the Lochiels, should have been trustworthy but who, like Glengarry, was so full of bitterness for what he and his family had suffered that he was ready to take government bribes.

The Glennevis family's long connection with the Gordons, strong supporters of the Whig government and therefore opposed to the Stuarts, is taken to be the reason why Alexander, Samuel's eldest brother, refused to rise for Prince Charles. Despite this, his younger brothers did fight for the Prince, ensuring the safety of their estates by being on both sides, a common precaution in civil wars. Alexander was imprisoned for about a year, Allan was killed at Culloden, and most of their relations fought for the Jacobites throughout the whole campaign. Subsequently deemed as traitors, the tide of persecution that followed the battle of Culloden descended with all its devastating brutality upon the members of their clan.

During Alexander's imprisonment his wife, a daughter of Cameron of Dungallon and thus Jean Cameron's sister, was the woman who, as already told, when hiding in a cave on Ben Nevis, was attacked and her child injured by a soldier's sword. Stripped of her own clothes down to her petticoat, she had to watch helplessly as the gold buttons and lace were ripped from her little boy's coat. Fortunately she had buried most things of value behind the garden wall, but Glennevis House, like Achnacarry, was sacked and burnt to the ground.

Alexander Cameron of Glennevis was released from Edinburgh Castle on 7th July 1746. Returning home he had launched himself into the cattle trade, buying beasts in large numbers to fatten and then sell on. Where did he get the money for this was a question that many asked. Commonly it was supposed that he had acquired some of the buried gold.

The Cumberland papers contain a memoir sent from someone in Scotland to the Duke's *aide-de-camp*, Colonel Napier. Having described what had happened to the money after its being put ashore by the French ships lying in Loch nan Uamh, the informant continued to explain how, on Prince Charles sailing for France, he had made Cluny MacPherson the custodian of the buried horde of *louis d'dors*. He then continued to describe how, following the Prince's departure, Cluny had immediately dug it up from the hiding places shown to him by Doctor Archie, and transferred it to Badenoch for greater safety, as he believed.

> And there were in company with him Angus Cameron of Downan, a Rannoch man, brother to Glennevis, and MacPherson of Breackachy a brother-in-law of his own, and his piper...[135]
>
> I know it is strongly suspected that Cameron of Glennevis, whose brother (*Angus*) was with Cluny at carrying away the 12,000, has received a large proportion by some means or other, and there is great reason to think so, as he was almost bankrupt before the rebellion and is now shewing away in a very different manner, particularly this year about a month ago, there were 120 Louis d'ors sent from him to a man in Locharkeek *(Loch Arkaig)* to buy cattle for him; and some of the Camerons having lately threatened to be resented of him for his

> behaviour about yt money, he met with them, and parted good friends, which is supposed to have been done by giving them considerably[136]

Napier's unknown correspondent then embarks on a lengthy story of how Cole, the code name for Major Kennedy, was supposed to land on the west coast to meet Cluny *'and carry away the money',* but he thinks that he actually landed on the east coast because Samuel Cameron, a Major in the regiment which was Lochiel's in the French Service, was at Edinburgh:

> And came in a chaise with the famous Mrs Jean Cameron to Stirling, where they parted, and she came to her house in Morvern about the middle of March, and he took a different route. It is supposed that he came over on a message with regard to that money. And I rather believe it as his two brothers seem to have been concerned in it.[137]

Confusion here sets in. Who does he mean by *'the famous Mrs Jean Cameron?'.* Is it to be taken that it was Archie's wife, or was she, as is generally believed, Jennie Cameron, one of the family of Glendessary who was widely and wrongly supposed to be Prince Charles's mistress? Jennie Cameron did have a house in Morvern, therefore it seems probable that she was the lady in the coach. The anonymous writer continues to affirm:

> It has been said that the French Officer came to Mrs Jean Cameron, but I am certain he has not come, else I would have got intelligence of him, for I have had a sharp look out for him and all others of that kind. And I think he would not probably venture so near the Command and specially after hearing of Barrisdale's fate. *(Barrisdale had been taken prisoner in March 1749).*

> It is said that his two brothers and Cluny have differed about the money, and therefore Cluny would not see this French Officer nor trust him with anything and some say he is gone back again, but how far this is true I can't possibly determine.
> The above is all that I have been able to learn with regard to that money from first to last, and I am much convinced that the substance of it is true. (unsigned)[138]

One can only conjecture, but the French officer he mentions is very likely to be Jennie's travelling companion, Samuel Cameron by name.

Archie was in fact at Douai, some forty kilometres from Lille, the seat of a Jesuit college and a haven for Jacobite spies. Proof lies in a letter, dated 11th June 1751, which he wrote from there to James Edgar telling him of the death of Sir William Gordon of Park, lieutenant colonel of Lord Ogilvie's regiment and suggesting that he, Archie, might be given the vacant post of lieutenant-colonel:

> which I enjoyed till, in October thereafter, I was made captain of Grenadiers in my brother's regiment, *(Albany's)* and ever since I got a company a second time, it is allowed by the most experienced officers of the army, that it is my due to be the oldest captain now, and as there is a lieutenant-colonel awanting, I cannot help being so vain as to think myself more entitled to it than any other in the regiment...If you think this proper, I wish you would apply to the king for a recommendation, to my Lord Clare and my Lord Ogilvie (who were always my good friends) towards naming me lieutenant-colonel. The principal advantage I propose by this is to be a means to procure me a retreat if at any time I see occasion for it according as things turn out, especially if the ball received at Falkirk, and is

> still in my body, gives me as much trouble as it did in winter and spring last, which helped the continuance of my sickness at that time, - I should propose, in case it may render me incapable of serving, to live in the way it may give me less trouble. However, I leave it to your prudence.[139]

But Doctor Archie did not achieve the coveted command of his regiment as far as any records show. All that is known is that at that time he and Jean, much impoverished, were worried about their children's education. William Drummond of Balhaldie came to their rescue. Jean had written to him to tell him of the arrival in France of their son Donald who had been living in the Drummond family house in Dunblane since 1746. It would seem that William Drummond, a personal friend of the Rector of the Scots College at Douai, persuaded him to give Jean's younger son Charles Cameron a place in the college, as is recorded in an entry in the diary dated 24th January 1752.

Meanwhile, if the evidence of the man who betrayed him can be trusted, Archie was then sent on a mission to Scotland by Prince Charles.

Chapter 39
THE ELIBANK PLOT

Prince Charles had visited London incognito in September 1750. Wearing *'an Abbés dress with a black patch over his eye and his eyebrows black'd'*, he had actually walked through the streets unnoticed. Looking at the defences of the Tower of London he had remarked to his companion, Colonel Brett, that a gate might be blown open with a petard.

This seems to have been the inspiration for what came to be known as *'The Elibank Plot'*, so named because the leading light behind it was a wild young man called Alexander Elibank, a younger brother of Lord Elibank. In the summer of 1751, charged with violence during the parliamentary election, Alexander was held in prison until, when released at the end of the session, he was carried in triumph to his brother's house in the Strand.

Once free he travelled to France where he assured Prince Charles that, *'in and about Westminster, he could raise five hundred men to fight for him'* on the strength of which a plan was formed. Alexander himself, with some officers from Lord Ogilvie's regiment, would come over from France to London where they would secretly assemble several hundred of the Prince's supporters. Charles would then join them and, on a given date, they would burst into St James's Palace to kill, or kidnap, George II and his family.

Most importantly, in addition to the Londoners, Alasdair Ruadh MacDonell, Young Glengarry, had assured him that he had *'above four hundred Brave Highlanders ready at my call'* to answer the call to arms.

Essential to the success of the whole mad enterprise was the possibility that General James Keith, the Earl Marischal's brother, in the service of the

King of Sweden, would land in Scotland with a Swedish army to support a simultaneous rising, led by Young Glengarry, and a combined force of the Camerons under young Lochiel's uncle, Archie Cameron.

It was for this purpose that, according to Glengarry, arrangements were made for his cousin MacDonald of Lochgarry and Archie Cameron to meet with the Prince at the little town of Menin in Flanders.

Glengarry, once assured of the details, was quick to pass them on to the source from which he hoped he would soon gain recompense. On 4th November 1752, he sat down to write to his *'special friend'* Henry Pelham, signing himself ALEXR. JEANSON, another of his alibis. In this letter he characteristically wrote the word 'who' as 'how'. The page, headed *Information,* betrays the Elibank Plot:

> The Young Pretender about the latter end of September (1752) sent Mr Murray *(of Elibank)* for Lochgarry and Doctor Archibald Cameron. They met him at Menin. He informed them that he hoped he had brought matters to such a bearing, particularly at the King of Prussia's Court, whom he expected in a short time to have a strong alliance with – that he did not desire the Highlanders to rise in Arms until General Keith *(brother of the Earl Marischal)* was landed in the North of Scotland with some troops. He likewise assur'd them that some of the greatest weight in England, 'tho' formerly great opposers to his family', were engaged in this attempt, and that he expected to meet with very little opposition. In consequence of this he gave Lochgarry, Doctor Cameron, Blairfety, Robertson of Wood Streat, Skalleter, mony; and sent them to Scotland, so as to meet several Highland gentlemen at the Crief Market for Black Cattel. Cameron, Cassifairn and Glenevegh were those how *(who)* were to carry on the Correspondence twixt the Southern Jacobites and Clunie MacPherson. Lochgary after the general meeting at Menin with the Young Pretender, was for two nights at Gent in Flanders. I

was at Boulogne when Sir James Harrison gave me directions to go to Gent, but to my great surprize as I lighted of horseback at Furnes was tipt' upon the shoulder by one Morrison *(Prince Charles's valet)* how desir'd me to stop for a little at the Inn. I was not long there when the Young Pretender enter'd my room. The discourse chiefly turn'd upon the Scheme in England, when he repeated the same assurance as to Lochgary, but in stronger terms, and with the addition that the Swedes were to embark at Gattenburgh *(Göthenburg),* and that Mr Murray was sent with commissions for me, and full instructions how I was to act in Scotland. The Young Chevalier was so positive of his schemes succeeding, that he told me he expected to be in London very soon himself, and that he was determin'd to give the present Government no quiet until he succeeded or dyed in the attempt. I came over here *(to England)* by his express orders; I waited on Lord Elibank who, after the strong assurances of the Young Pretender, surprised me to the greatest degree, by telling me that all was put off for some time, and that his brother *(Murray)* had repassd the seas in order to aquent the Young Pretender of it, and from him he was to go straight to Paris to Lord Marishal. It is not above nine days since I left the Young Pretender at Furnes...Its not above five days since Mr Murray left London. Probably the landing for England was to be from France, as there is 12,000 troops in Flanders more than the ordinary compliment. This the Comon French takes notice off. But I can say nothing of this with certainty. The Young Chevalier has more than once seen the King of Prussia, but none other of his Court, that ever I could learn but General Keith, Sir John Douglas, Mr Charteris *(Lord Elcho's brother)* and Hepburn of Keith, are in the secret. The Young Chevalier has been in close correspondence with England for a year and a halph past. Mr Carte the Historian has carried frequent messages. They never commit anything in writing. Elderman Hethcot is principall Manager. The very words the Young Pretender told me was that all

> this scheme was laid and transacted by Whiggers, that no Roman Catholic was concerned, and obliged me to give my word and honour that I would write nothing concerning him or his plan to Rome. After what I said last night this is all that occurs to me at present. I will lose no time in my transactions, and I will take care they will allways be conforme to your directions, and as I have throwen myself entirely upon you, I am determined to run all hazards upon this occasion, which I hope will entitle me to your favour and his Majesty's protection.[140]

Improbable as was the information contained in Young Glengarry's letter, the Government took it seriously. That there was some truth in what he had written emerged when it was discovered that both Archie Cameron and Donald MacDonald of Lochgarry were in Scotland, whence they had sailed from Ostend. Two frigates were sent out to intercept them, so it is claimed, but somehow they managed to come ashore on the West Coast of Scotland.[141]

Soon reports filtered in of conversations that Cameron was said to have had with various people in the Highlands sometime during the winter of 1752-3.

` James Mor MacGregor, Rob Roy's eldest son, in his confession made in London on 6th November 1753 said that, in preparation for renewed rebellion, 9,000 stands of arms had been lodged in Clanranald's country, but that Doctor Cameron had taken away, without orders, 250 Stands. He also claimed that, while in the Isle of Man he had met an Irishman, a Mr Savage, who had been told by Sir Archibald Stewart of Castle Milk, near Greenock, that he had seen Doctor Cameron in Stirlingshire, who had informed him:

> that he hoped the Restoration would happen soon, for that preparations were making for it, and that he had been sent to Scotland to conduct some affairs for that purpose.[142]

That the information was passed on to Samuel Cameron, possibly through Murray of Broughton, must remain speculation but, in view of their known correspondence, it seems probable.

Charles Erskine, the Lord Justice Clerk, who having recently dealt with Jean Cameron thought her an honest lady, believed there was no real cause for alarm, but nonetheless added in a report to the Duke of Newcastle:

> that the clansmen are divided amongst themselves, which is a consolation, but whether a common *mischief* might not bring them to unite I cannot answer.

Archie reputedly just escaped capture on one occasion but, warned in time by watchful Jacobites, avoided the trap that was set for him.[143] He was thought, however, to have been in Scotland over the winter of 1752-3 and must surely have heard, with great sadness, of the murder of his cousin, Colin Campbell of Glenure, by an assassin who has never been named.

Colin, an exceptionally handsome man, the son of Campbell of Barcaldine in Appin, had married the daughter of Lord Reay. Given Glenure, at the head of Glen Creran by his father, he had been made factor of the Jacobites' forfeited estates. Riding down from the Ballachulish Ferry into Appin to evict attainted tenants from their farms, he was shot with a long barrelled rifle by a marksman hiding on the hill. The case, tried in Inveraray and presided over by the Lord Chief Justice, Archibald, Duke of Argyll, caused a great sensation in the country.

The murderer was never caught but an Appin farmer, James Stewart of the Glen, found guilty of being an accessory to the crime, was condemned to death.

Made a scapegoat, he was executed close to the Ballachulish Ferry where, as a warning of what others hostile to the government might expect, his body was left hanging in chains.

Doctor Archie should have been warned; the tragedy of the Appin Murder, as it came to be called, was an example of what anyone deemed a traitor could expect. But, obedient to Prince Charles's order, he was certainly back in Scotland by February 1753.

He found the country much changed, even since his brief visit of four years before. Immediately following the Rising of 1745 the draconian legislation of the Government, which was to change the social status of the Highlands, was now taking effect. Determined to subdue the power of the Highland chiefs, held largely responsible for supporting Prince Charles, the Parliament of 1746 had almost stripped them of their powers. Heritable jurisdictions had been abolished while the Tenures Abolition Act had ended the military tenures (by which tacksmen, or tenants, were obliged to obey a summons to arms) by converting them into feu holdings.

The sudden change in authority was causing much confusion. People who through inbred loyalty had accepted the ruling of their chief, were in some cases finding it auspicious to curry favour with the new administration. By the early spring of 1753 the government in London, probably thanks to Young Glengarry, knew that Archie Cameron was in Scotland.

Archie himself was certainly aware of this. Having narrowly escaped capture on one occasion, he was constantly on the watch. Seen in the light of hereafter he should certainly have been more circumspect but, if not his own relations, who else should he trust? Thus it was that when he met Samuel Cameron of Glennevis, he thought him to be totally reliable to the point where he asked him if he knew of a safe house in which, for a time, he could live.

Samuel Cameron, of all people, should have been dependable, his eldest brother being married to Mary Cameron of Dungallon, the doctor's sister-in-law. Although Archie may have been aware that 'Crookshanks' had been ingrained from childhood with resentment against the family of Lochiel, he would never have thought for an instant that, embittered against the Stuarts, he was now a Government spy.

In *The Gentleman's Magazine* for 1747 it is recorded that, on Tuesday 7th July, Alexander MacDonald of Kingsburgh and Alexander Cameron of Glennevis were discharged from Edinburgh Castle.[144] Alexander, Samuel's eldest brother, most probably as part of an agreement by which he obtained his release, is believed to have imparted such knowledge of the movements and plans of the defeated Jacobites as he then possessed.

A paper in the Scottish Records Office, written by an anonymous informer to the government, who by his spelling and classical references was obviously a literate man, states that Glennevis got 3,000 of the gold buried at Loch Arkaig,[145]` this being a reason, he adduced, for added animosity between the Glennevis Camerons and Cluny MacPherson.

Despite the fact that his brother appears to have got some of the French gold Samuel, when discharged from the Prince's army, was left homeless and without any form of income. Faced with destitution, he had succumbed to the government's offer of money in return for information on any of the insurgents believed to be still at large.

Was he in touch with Young Glengarry? Bearing in mind that, as near neighbours, the two must have known each other as boys and young men, this does seem likely although, unless further evidence emerges, it remains impossible to prove. Judging by his known actions, however, it seems plain that Samuel Cameron, succumbing to rancour and poverty, had joined the network of spies promised recompense for information on the whereabouts of wanted Jacobites by the British government.

Somehow, somewhere, he came across Archie in February 1753. The small, bandy-legged figure being instantly recognizable, Archie was probably pleased to see him if only to hear news of both his family and mutual friends. Perhaps the two of them found an ale house in which to warm themselves before a fire and share a dram. In that atmosphere it would have been so easy to forget old animosities and, for a moment, for Archie to drop his guard. But whatever the circumstances of their meeting, Archie took Samuel into his confidence, telling him that he meant to stay in Scotland until May or June, *'but if nothing happened in that time he would never credit any promise on behalf of the Pretender'.*[146]

This, if Samuel was telling the truth, infers that plans for a rising had not been entirely abandoned by the Prince's supporters in England. Also it points the question as to whether Archie was *'stirring up the Highlands'* as Young Glengarry, betraying him, so fatally claimed.

Archie asked Samuel if he knew of a safe house where he could stay, his present accommodation being in some way unsatisfactory. Samuel then suggested Brenachoile, a house on Loch Katrine in the Trossachs belonging to Stewart of Glenbuckie which, as he pointed out, was not only remote but, being far from Cameron land was unlikely to be searched by the soldiers still scouring the country for rebels.

Archie jumped at the suggestion. Never did it even occur to him that Samuel, his cousin, was already working out the fastest way by which this gold nugget of information could be used to his own benefit.

Chapter 40
BRENACHOILE

John Stewart of Glenbuckie had bought the property of Glen Buckie from his brother-in-law, whose family had held the wide glen on the south shore of Loch Voil in Perthshire from the beginning of the 16th century. Descended from the Stewarts of Ardshiel in Appin, John was loyal to the Jacobite cause.

His house of Breneachyll (Brenachoile) on the north-east side of Loch Katrine, as the crow flies some twenty miles over the hills from the head of Glen Buckie, had already been used as a hiding place for Lord John Murray, brother of the Duke of Perth, when he was 'skulking' in the Highlands in the spring of 1744. Considered a 'safe house' it should have been an ideal place for Archie to hide, lying in a remote location in an area where he was unknown.

But one thing he did not realize (and which Samuel undoubtedly concealed) was that the barracks at Inversnaid, on the east bank of Loch Lomond, were only some six miles away over the hills from the south-west shore of Loch Katrine.

Said to have been in disguise and presumably wearing the despised hodden grey, ordered by the government to replace the forbidden Highland dress, and a dark wig, Archie pretended to be something other than a doctor, possibly a cattle dealer of which there were plenty around, and going by the name of Mr Chalmers (the name he had always used when 'under cover'). A kindly man, who spoke in their native Gaelic, he soon made friends with the people of the little farming townships lying close to Loch Katrine. Some of them however, guessed him to be a hunted rebel. Keen to save him they organized an alarm system by which the children were told to watch out for soldiers and tell the gentleman at *an-tigh-mor* (the big house) if any redcoats came in sight.

For young Captain Craven, in command of a detachment of Lord Guise's Regiment, life in the barracks of Inversnaid in the month of March was exceedingly dull. With nothing to look at but the towering, snow-capped mass of Ben Lomond above him and the ice fringed water of Loch Lomond in front, he passed the time in drilling his men and playing cards with his junior officers with whom he enlivened the evening by sharing a dram or two.

As ever the big excitement of the week was the arrival of the young soldier who had ridden from Stirling with the mail. The men of the garrison gathered round eagerly as he unloaded his saddle-bags. There were letters for Captain Craven, including one labelled top secret, which he hastened to open in his office well away from prying eyes.

It told him that a dangerous traitor, Doctor Archibald Cameron by name, had been reported as being in hiding in a house called Brenachoile on Loch Katrine. The missive included an order to arrest him by any possible means. Captain Craven was young, but by no means a fool. With the twelve men whom he could muster, starting at first light the following morning, he marched along the shore of Loch Arklet to reach the west side of Loch Katrine. On the other side a low grey house, built of granite, stood above a stretch of meadow running down to Loch Katrine.

Marching in single file round the foot of the loch, moving quietly with bent shoulders in the hopes of being unobserved, they saw that the building, which from the distance had seemed deserted, must be occupied by someone, for a thin stream of smoke rose from one of the chimneys into the lightening sky. Before them lay one of the farming townships, a cluster of thatched cottages from whence came the lowing of cattle, the cackle of hens and the loud barking of dogs. Approaching, they saw a little girl run away from one of the cottages that formed the communal group.

Craven guessed correctly that she was going to raise the alarm. Ordering his men to run after her, he too pursued the diminutive fleeing figure, her white smock giving her away. She ran with the speed of a hare, amazing for one so small. Then on reaching the next small hamlet they saw her dash into a hut from which a boy then bolted like a dog freed from its leash.

'After him' shouted Craven, *'do not let him get away'.*

His men pursued, until getting within gunshot of the running boy they levelled their muskets, yelling at him to stop or they would fire. The words spoken in English were beyond his comprehension, but he understood their meaning at sight of the levelled guns. Halting until the soldiers reached him, he was then somehow made to realize that the men in redcoats would not kill him if he led the way to Brenachoile.

Coming within view of the house, seeing smoke now rising faster from what he thought might be the kitchen chimney, Captain Craven deduced that his quarry was at home. He also guessed shrewdly what might happen next so that, dividing his men into two parties, he sent six of them to the front of the building and the other six to the rear.

It happened as he had anticipated. Doctor Archie, escaping from a back window, was caught as he tried to run towards the cover of a wood. Overpowered he surrendered without a struggle to be led back to the house.

Although thoroughly searched by the soldiers under Captain Craven's watchful eye, no form of incriminating evidence was found. Thereafter, Archie was marched back to Inversnaid Barracks, his captors before and behind him as well as on either side. The last part of the distance was covered in near darkness, the party arriving at the Barracks at about two o'clock in the morning, in the words of the triumphant Captain Craven, *'heartily tired having waded through rivers and bogs up to my knees, and passed some rough rocky mountains, but the satisfaction of succeeding makes it rather a pleasure'.*[147]

From there Archie was taken prisoner to Stirling. By the laws of the government he was termed a rebel and his name, included in the Act of Attainder passed in 1746, had been excluded from the Act of Indemnity of the following year. His reason for not appearing to swear fealty to King George was that *'in 1746, he came from France to surrender himself, agreeable to the Proclamation, but was prevented by an Accident happening in his Family'.*[148] Under these circumstances he knew that he would have no chance of defending himself if found in Scotland, and that his sentence of death would certainly follow unless the Government showed mercy.

In Stirling Castle he was identified, by two independent witnesses, as the person mentioned in the Act of Attainder. On the next day he was taken to Edinburgh. Reaching the city he was escorted up to the castle from the Grassmarket as crowds gathered to watch, some to jibe, some to silently sympathize with this quietly dressed, plainly unarmed and harmless man.

Received by the governor at the castle, he was told that as a state prisoner he would be held under strict supervision within one of the cells. Privilege would not be granted to a traitor. Hearing these words he knew, with an awful certainty, that in his case there would be no chance of escape. The cold and the darkness engulfed him as he heard the turning of the key.

The following day in Edinburgh Castle he was examined by James Erskine, Lord Grange, the Lord Justice Clerk, who reported that *'he seemed in great concern'* but yet would give nothing away, maintaining that he had come to Scotland purely on private matters. Erskine warned him *'of the dangerous precipice on which he stood, if he did not by some very material discovery open a door to let in hopes of his majesty's innate clemency'.* Erskine wondered if he might be encouraged to say more if he were to be *'examined in more awful presence'.* The Duke of Newcastle agreed with this suggestion and on 4th April he was sent under strong escort, probably travelling in one of the coaches which ran between the two capitals, to London.

Chapter 41
THE INFORMER

On word of Doctor Archie's arrest reaching London Young Glengarry, who had sworn to Pelham that he would not be in touch with Rome, immediately picked up his pen.

Writing to James Edgar from Arras, in Flanders, dating his letter 5th April 1753, he referred to the postponement of the Elibank plot in the previous November:

> Thank God the Prince did not venture himself then at London. Tho he was upon the Coast ready at a Call to put himself at their head. I wish he may not be brought to venture sow far, upon the stress laid upon a sudden blow, to be done by the English; we will see if the month of May or June will produce something more effective than Novr., and I am sorry to aquent you that the sow great stress laid upon these projects is lick to prove fatal to some, for Lochgary and Doctor Archibald Cameron, were sent to the Highlands to prepair the Clans to be in readiness: thire beeing sent was much against my opinion, as I always ensisted, and will always persist, that no stir should be done until the English would be so farr engaged that they could not draw back. I hope his Majesty will approve of my conduct in this. Doctor Cameron was taken by a party of soldiers in Boruder*(?)* and is now actually secured in the Castel of Edinr. Loch*(garry)* still remains but what his fate will be is very precarious. The concert in Novr. was that I was to remain in London, as I had above four hundred brave Highlanders ready at my call, and after matters had broke out there to sett off directly for Scotland as no raising would be made amongst the Clans without my presence...I believe in a few days that I will take a private

start to London, tho' I am still so weake after my leate Illness at Paris that I am scarce yet able to undergo much fatigue. I have left directions with Mr Gordon, principal of the Scots College, to forward any letters for me to a friend at Boulogne, how has a secure way of trading by ships and Letters to me. I will be very glad to hear from you particularly as I Expect to return in a few weeks back to France. I have one favour to ask of you, and I hope it wont displease his Majesty. Its, that whatever I write upon this topick, be neither shown or communicated to any other person, as there reports that people with you communicate their Intelligence too freely to the Court of france, which you know may go farther, and prove of dangerous consequence. I hope the freedom with which I express myself will be wholly attributed to the warmth of my zeal for the good of the cause, and I beg you'l forgive the hurry I am in writing this, and I rely upon your friendship to Excuse the same towards his Majesty in case you think Proper to lay this hurried scrawl before him, for what with the fatigue of posting and Other Affairs, I am so Tumbled. I wish with all my heart you may conceve the sincer true and ready sentiments which Induced me to write so freely, and as the Gentilman with whom I send this to Paris is just ready to set off, I beg you allow me to conclude, and I hope you'll not faile to lay me at his Majesty's and Royal Emmency's feet and at the same time Believe me Sir

Your most obedient and most humble Servt

MACKDONELL.[149]

In London, on 27th April 1753 Horace Walpole, son of the late Prime Minister wrote to his friend the British Consul in Florence, Sir Horace Mann:

What you say you have heard of strange conspiracies, fomented by our nephew *(The King*

> *of Prussia)* is not entirely groundless. A Doctor Cameron has been seized in Scotland, who certainly came over with commission to feel the ground. He is brought to London... Intelligence has been received some time before of his intended journey to Britain, with a commission from Prussia to offer arms to the disaffected Highlanders, at the same time that ships were hiring in the north to transport men.
> The fairness of Doctor Cameron's character, compared with the severity he received from a government most laudably mild to its enemies, confirmed this report. That Prussia, which opened its inhospitable arms to every British rebel, should have tampered in such a business was by no means improbable. The King hated his uncle: but could a Protestant potentate dip in designs for restoring a popish government?[150]

From this it can be taken that the British government feared that rebellion would break out again in Scotland with military aid supplied by King Frederick of Prussia. Glengarry's letter indicates that some such thing was planned in the months of May or June.

On the evidence of the letters quoted, and of what Archie supposedly said to Samuel Cameron about staying in Scotland until May or June, it would seem that he was waiting for some form of insurrection to begin.

On 2nd May, after nothing had been heard of Archie for some months young Edgar, in Lille, wrote desperately to his father in Rome:

> We have no account of Cameron except by the Gazete. It is thought that all the others who have been apprehended either had of the Princes's money in their hands, of that the Government expects they can make some discoveries about it; I wish with all my heart the Gov. had got it in

> the beginning, for it has given the greatest stroke to the cause that can be imagined, it has divided the different clans more than ever, and even those of the same clan and family; so that they are ready to destroy and betray one another. Altho I have not altered my opinion about Mr M. *(Murray of Broughton)* yet as he may on an occasion be of great use to the cause with the Londoners – I thought it not amiss to write him a line to let him know the regard you had for him, for as I know him to be vastly vain and full of himself I thought this might be a spur to his zeale.[151]

Prince Charles, told of Doctor Archie's arrest, jumped to the conclusion that someone in France had betrayed him. Writing to the Earl Marischal on 13th April, he said:

> I am extremely unesi by the accident that has happened to a Certain person. You know how much I was against people in that Service. My antipathy, iff possible, increses every day, which makes me absolutely determined whatever happens never to approach their Country *(France)* or have to do with anibody that comes with them.[152]

Fearful for his own safety, he then shortly moved to Cologne.

Chapter 42
THE TOWER OF LONDON

Archie Cameron arrived in London on 16th April, the seventh anniversary of the battle of Culloden. Imprisoned in the Tower, he was probably held in the Lieutenant's lodgings where, over the centuries, so many political prisoners had been held.

As was customary he, or members of his family, were expected to pay the then considerable sum of £4 a week both for his own keep and that of the two warders to whom his safety was assigned.

Examined by the Privy Council on the day after his arrival, he revealed nothing of any importance except for one curious interchange with the Duke of Newcastle, who asked why he had made such a long and expensive visit to Rome. Archie honestly and plainly answered:

> *'I went to see my old master, and to receive his commands for my young master'*. 'And did you see your young master lately?' Newcastle asked. *'Yes'* was the answer. 'Where did you see him?' continued his inquisitor. *'At Paris',* Archie Cameron replied. (Here a considerable pause was made and orders were given to write down exactly the words of the Doctor, they imagining some mighty discovery to be made by him.) Then it was asked 'When did you see your young master, as you call him, last in Paris?' *'In 1748'* said Archie calmly. They were much enraged at this answer, as they conjectured the doctor would have condescended upon some time later, viz: in 1751 or 1752. The Duke of Newcastle, in particular, was so provoked that he stormed furiously out of the room bawling out 'This is the height of insolence! Most insufferable insolence! Insolence not to be borne with!' Etc. etc. In a word such was the blustering that Dr Cameron (as he acknowledged to a particular friend) was almost ready to smile, even in the presence of the Council.[153]

Further witnesses were found in London who could identify Cameron, and on the day following his interrogation by the Privy Council he was brought before the King's Bench and sentenced to death by hanging. It was noticed that *'he heard his sentence without any alteration of countenance, except that his lips closed and his mouth began to fill and he made three or four very low reverences to the bench when he retired.*[154]

Initially only one concession was allowed, that of his execution being postponed till 7th June so that his wife Jean might come over from France to join him for a few days.

Archie was granted this dispensation on his explaining to the authorities that *'he had seven children who, with his wife, were all dependent upon him, and his not seeing her would be worse for him than death itself'.*[155]

Someone, or perhaps several amongst them, must have pitied the family's situation. Permission was granted for Jean to travel so that, leaving the two year old baby James in the care of friends, or perhaps his older siblings, she sailed for England immediately.

She arrived in London on 29th May. Eight months pregnant, she was heavy with child. Nonetheless, so paranoid were the government authorities over fear of a renewed Jacobite rising, that on her arrival she was lodged with her husband in the Tower.

Her feelings and those of her husband at their reunion under these circumstances are, as his contemporary biographer, Alexander Henderson, writes so poignantly, almost beyond all words:

> ...who received her with all that Tenderness and Affection, which the Greatness and Solemnity of the Occasion could inspire. The Grief and Anguish of her soul is much more easily imagined than described. She came to take her

> last Farewel of him, who, by all the Ties of mutual Affection, was dearer to her than all the World. And as an Aggravation to her Affliction, she not only saw herself about to be deprived of an affectionate Husband, but to be left destitute of a Support for herself and her numerous Family. Their Children, the dear Pledges of their Love, must now be exposed to all the Necessities and Casualties of Life, without the Patronage of a kind and indulgent Father, to have recourse to for Advice and Assistance. The Consideration of this Train of Evils, now hastening upon her, made such a strong Impression on her Mind, as to force a Flood of Tears from her mournful Eyes. The Doctor comforted her as well as he could, and desired her to use all the Means in her Power to save his Life, which was to present a Petition in his Favour to his Majesty, who, perhaps, might be prevailed upon to save him.[156]

Jean did everything humanly possible. Allowed out of the Tower, she made her way to St James's Palace where, according to tradition, hugely pregnant as she was, she threw herself at the feet of the King, begging him to save her husband's life. More factually she is known to have handed in petitions to both King George and his daughter-in-law, Caroline of Brunswick, the popular Princess of Wales. She also wrote to the few other people whom she knew in London to beg them to do anything and everything they could to prevent Archie's execution.

She was not alone in her struggle. As news of Doctor Archie's arrest reached France, the French government instructed their ambassador in London, the Duc de Mirepoix, to ensure his release on the grounds that he was a serving officer in the army of their Most Christian King, as a colonel of the Regiment d'Albany and as a captain of the Foot. King James, in deepest concern over the fate of the man he had seen so recently in Rome and of whose loyalty he was totally convinced, wrote personally to Cardinal Portocarrero asking him to draw the attention of José de Carvajal, King Ferdinand's chief minister (with whom Pelham's ministry had been on friendly terms since the signing of the Anglo-Spanish Treaty of Madrid in 1750) to Cameron's danger, emphasizing that he was a colonel in the service of the Most Catholic King. The Duke of Argyll was also approached, but professed himself quite unable to do anything. (see note No.171)

But all attempts to save Doctor Archie failed. Henry Pelham, who had so recently been assured by *'his special friend'* Young Glengarry that Doctor Archie had been *'stirring up the Highlands'* to renewed rebellion, bent the ear of the King to tell him that the mild mannered Scotsman was a danger to the state. King George believed him, remarking only that it now seemed a long time since the Act of Amnesty had been passed and that too much blood had already been shed. Reluctant to sign the death warrant, he allowed himself to be convinced that it was necessary, stipulating only, perhaps on the pleas of Jean Cameron if he actually heard them at all, that the sentence be reduced to hanging. Thus Archie was spared the dreadful medieval punishment of a traitor of being hung drawn and quartered, his entrails thrown into a fire while he was still alive.

Chapter 43
THE BLUNT PENCIL

Held in the Tower of London and constantly watched by two warders, Doctor Archie was treated as a criminal as he himself describes. Denied writing materials, he managed to find some slips of paper on which, undetected when it was growing dark, he wrote, on the first slip of paper:

Tower, 6th June, 1753

> Being denied the use of pen, ink, and paper, (except in the presence of one or more officers who always took away the paper from me, when I began to write my complaints) and not even allowed the use of a knife, with which I might cut a poor blunted pencil, that had escaped the diligence of my searchers I have notwithstanding, as I could find opportunity, attempted to set down on some slips of paper, in as legible characters as I was able, what I would have my country satisfied of, with regard to myself and the cause in which I am now going to lay down my life.
>
> As to my religion, I thank God I die a member, (tho' unworthy), of that church in whose communion I have always lived, *the Episcopal Church of Scotland*, as by law established before the *most unnaturall Rebellion* began in 1688, which for the sins of these nations hath continued to this day: and I firmly trust to find, at the most awful and impartial tribunal of the Almighty King of Kings, through the merits of my Blessed Lord and Saviour Jesus Christ, that mercy (tho' undeserved) to my immortal part which is here denied to my earthly by an *usurper* and his *faction*, tho' it be well known I have been the instrument in preventing the ruin and destruction of many of my poor deluded countrymen who were in their service, as I shall make appear before I have done, if opportunities of writing fail me not.

On the second slip of paper:

> In order to convince the world of the uprightness of my intentions while in the Prince of Wales's army, as well as to shew the *cruelty, injustice, and ingratitude* of my murderers, I think it my proper duty in the first place to take notice how much better usage I might have expected of my country, if humanity and good nature were now looked upon with the same eyes as in the time of our brave and generous ancestors; but I'm sorry to observe that our present men in power are so far sunk below the noble spirit of the ancient Britons, as hardly at this day to be distinguished from the very basest of mankind. Nor could the present possessor of the throne of our *injured sovereign*, if he looked on himself as the father and natural prince of this country, suffer the life of one to be taken away who has saved the lives and effects of more than 300 persons in Scotland, who were firmly attached to him and his party; but it seems it is now made a crime to save the lives of Scotchmen.
>
> As neither the time nor the poor materials I have for writing, will allow me to descend to a particular enumeration of all the services I have done to the friends of the Usurper, I shall therefore only mention a few names of the most known and such as can be well attested.
>
> In July, 1745, soon after the setting up of the Royal Standard, and before our small army had reached Corryarick, it was moved by some of the chiefs to apply to the Prince for a strong detachment of clans to distress Campbell of Invera's house and tenants in the neighbourhood which my brother Lochiel and I so successfully opposed, by representing to our generous leader (who was always an enemy to oppression) that such proceeding could be no way useful to his undertaking, that the motion was entirely laid aside, to the no small mortification of the

> proposer. My brother and I likewise prevented such another design against Braidalbin, to the great satisfaction of our dear Prince. And on our return from England to Glasgow
>
> Archibald Cameron.

On the third slip of paper:

> My brother and I did service to the town of Glasgow, of which the principal gentry in the neighbourhood were then, and are to this day very sensible, if they durst own the truth. But that might be construed as disaffection to a government founded on and supported by lies and falshood.
>
> On our march to Stirling, I myself (tho' I'm like to meet with a Hanoverian reward for it) hindered the whole town of Kirkintulloch from being destroyed and its inhabitants put to the sword by my brother's men, who were justly incensed against it for the inhuman murder of two of Lady Lochiel's servants but two months before. Here was a sufficient pretence for vengeance, had I been inclined to cruelty, but I thank God nothing was ever further from my nature, tho' I may have been otherwise represented. Mr Campbell of Shawfield likewise owes me some small favours done to himself and family, which at least deserve some return in my behalf.
>
> And Lady Duncan Campbell of Lochnell, now in London, can, if she pleases, vouch for the truth of some of the above facts.
>
> Archibald Cameron

On the fourth slip of paper

6th June 1753

I thank kind Providence I had the happiness to be early educated in the principles of Christian loyalty, which as I grew in years inspired me with an utter abhorrence of rebellion and usurpation, tho' ever so successful. And when I arrived at man's estate I had the testimony both of religion and reason to confirm me in the truth of my first principles. Thus my attachment to the Royal Family is more the result of examination and conviction than of prepossession and prejudice. And as I am now, so was I then, ready to seal my loyalty with my blood. As soon therefore as the royal youth had set up the king his father's standard, I immediately as in duty bound repaired to it, and as I had the honour from that time to be almost constantly about his person till November, 1748, (excepting the short time after the affair of Culloden that his Royal Highness was in the Western Isles), I became more and more captivated with his amiable and princely virtues, which are indeed in every instance so eminently great as I want words to describe.

I can farther affirm (and my present situation and that of my dear Prince too, can leave no room to suspect me of flattery) that as I have been his companion in the lowest degrees of adversity that ever prince was reduced to, so I have I beheld him too, as it were, on the highest pinacle of glory, amidst the continual applauses, and, I had almost said adorations, of the most brilliant court in Europe, yet he was always the same, ever affable and courteous, giving constant proofs of his great humanity and of his love for his friends and his country. What great good to these actions might not be expected from such a Prince, were he in possession of the throne of his ancestors! And as to his courage!

None that have everheard of his glorious attempt in 1745, can, I should think, call it in question. I cannot pass by in silence that most unjust and horrid calumny (viz. of giving no quarter to our enemy) raised by the rebels under the command of the *inhuman son* of the Elector of Hanover, which served as an excuse for the *unparalleled butchery*, committed by his orders in cold blood after the unhappy affair of Culloden, which, if true, must have come to my knowledge, who had the honour to serve my ever dear master in the quality of one of his *aides-de-camp*. And I hearby declare I never heard of such orders. This above is truth.

Archibald Cameron

I likewise declare on the word of a dying man that the last time I had the honour to see his Royal Highness, Charles, Prince of Wales, he told me from his own mouth, and bid me assure his friends from him *that he was a member of the Church of England.*

Archibald Cameron

On the fifth slip of paper:

To cover the cruelty of murdering me at this distance of time from passing *the unjust attainder*, I am accused of being deeply concerned in a new plot against the government (which if I was, neither the fear of the worst death their malice could invent nor the blustering and noisy threatnings of the tumultuous council, nor much less their flattering promises, could have extorted any discovery of it from me) but not so much as one evidence was ever produced to make good the charge. But it is my business to submit, since God in his all-wise Providence thinks fit to suffer it to be so. And I the more chearfully resign my life as it is taken away for doing my duty to God, my king and my country;

nor is there anything in this world I could so much wish to have it prolonged for, as to have another opportunity of employing the remainder of it in the same *glorious cause.*

Archibald Cameron

I thank God I was not in the least daunted at hearing the *bloody sentence* which my *unrighteous judge* pronounced with a seeming insensibility till he came to these words '*But not till you are dead'*, before which he made a pause, and uttering them with a particular emphasis, stared me full in the face to see, I suppose, if I was as much frightened at them as he perhaps would have been had he been in my place. As to the guilt he said I had to answer for, as having been instrumental in the *loss of so many lives*, let him and his constituents see to that. *At their hands, not at mine, will all the blood that had been shed on that account be required*.

God of His infinite mercy grant they may prevent the punishment which hangs over their heads by a sincere and timely repentance, and speedily return to their duty.

I pray God to hasten the restoration of the Royal Family (without which this miserably divided nation can never enjoy peace and happiness), and that it may please him to preserve and defend the King, the Prince of Wales, and the Duke of York from the power and malice of their enemies; to prosper and reward all my friends and benefactors, and to forgive all my enemies, murderers and false accusers, from the Elector of Hanover and his bloody son, down to Samuel Cameron the basest of their spies, as I freely do from the bottom of my heart. *(Sic subscribitur),*

Archibald Cameron.

I am now ready to be offered:
I have fought a good fight,
All glory be to God.[157]

And added at the foot by his widow:

> The above is a faithful transcript of my late dear husband's dying sentiments. *(Sic subscribitur),* Jean Cameron.

With all that was left of his stump of pencil he wrote one last letter to his son on the day before he died:

> Tower of London June 6th 1753
>
> My dear child,
>
> It is with the highest satisfaction that I have for some time past observed in you a sense of Honour and Loyalty Much beyond what could have been expected from a Boy of your years, and tho' Death will soon deprive Me of the Power of being of farther Service to my King, Prince & Country, yet what greatly adds to My Satisfaction is the Principle you shew in Your Letter to your Mother on the news of My being in Custody and the confidence you have of my inviolable Fidelity to the Royal Cause. I give you the Joy to assure you that your Confidence is well grounded; for I have been unalterable even in the Smallest Matters and my Approaching Death and the Most Severe Usage will rather Serve to confirm than Shake my fixed Resolution of remaining So for ever.
>
> I am far less concerned about Myself than about My Friends and ruined Country. They, not I, claim Pity, tho' I fall victim to Truth, Honour, and Uprightness, by the Rage of Hanoverian Councils, the declared Enemies to every Virtue. I thank God I am hearty, and in much better Health than I have been for some Years past, more especially since I saw that Letter which gives me such Hopes of your future Conduct, from the desire you express in it, that I should rather sacrifice my Life than save it on

> Dishonourable Terms. *(Macht mur in d'hair* – as Rothie used to say - *i.e. The son is like the Father).* I thank my God I was always easier ashamed than Frightened.
>
> I have no Money to leave you as a Legacy, but take what is of infinite more value viz: Above all things first serve God, next your King, Prince and country; then be always in your Duty to your Mother, Brothers and Sister; act honourably and honestly by your Neighbour; meddle in no Party Quarrels, but when you are personally Wrong'd, demand Justice with Coolness, Regularity & Resolution, without personal Reflections. Beware of ever Speaking to the Disadvantage of the Absent even tho' they should deserve it.
>
> I recommend to you in a Particular Manner the care of your Health. Observe great Moderation in Eating, at any rate Abstain from hearty and late Suppers; and, above all, Avoid Drinking and Whoring. Be a good oeconomist of Your little Money & Cloaths. Let the Company you frequent be rather of your Betters than Your Inferiors.
>
> My time and writing implements allow me only to recommend My most hearty Thanks to My noble and Worthy Colonel. Don't Neglect your Duty to him.
>
> My Love and dying Benediction to my Children, Affection to my Brother's Children, best wishes to all my Friends,and hearty Compliments to all My Good Acquaintance and ......[158]

Here the lead pencil finally ran out and Bishop Forbes, in his book, appended the following:

> Here this great, good man was obliged to leave off, probably for want of a knife to cut his bit of a pencil, and he never had another opportunity to add what he had to say any farther to his son, except what he told a friend by word of mouth,

the morning of his execution, in delivering him the last present he sent his son, which was a pair of steel shoe-buckles, with the charge (which, that it might not be forgotten, he repeated several times) viz:

'These I send by you to my wife as my last present to my son, and bid her tell him from me that I send him these and not my silver ones, and that if I had gold ones I would not send him the gold, But the steel ones which I wore when skulking for as steel is hard and of small value it is an emblem of constancy and disinterestedness. So I would have him constant and disinterested in the service and defence of his King, Prince and country and neither be bribed nor frightened from his duty'.[159]

Chapter 44
LAST TO DIE FOR THE JACOBITE CAUSE

Jean and Archie Cameron said goodbye to each other on the evening of 6th June when she was forced to leave the Tower. At ten o'clock on the following morning he was moved, with an escort of soldiers, onto Tower Green, where he was handed over to the Sheriff. He was wearing a light coloured coat, red waistcoat and breeches and a new bag-wig. He was then bound on a hurdle and drawn by four horses to the place of execution at Tyburn (now Marble Arch) where he arrived at a quarter past twelve. After joining with the clergyman, who accompanied him in the commendatory prayer, Archie said farewell to him and, as he seemed to stumble as he went down the steps from the cart, called after him in a cheerful voice *'Take care how you go, I think you do not know this way as well as I do'.*[160] He then made a present of money to the executioner and was immediately turned off. The body was allowed to hang on the gallows for three quarters of an hour and was then cut down. As it was not the Government's wish that he should be dismembered after death, his body was handed over to an undertaker and later taken secretly to the Strand where it was buried in the Queen's Chapel of the Savoy in the presence of four of his friends. Archie Cameron was forty-six years of age at the time of his death.

The Reverend Mr William Abernethie sent the following letter to Bishop Forbes:

> Poor Dr Cameron! – I believe I should say Happy Dr Cameron! – for never did man make a more glorious exit. He met the last great enemy with as much intrepidity and as much decency as even the great Balmerino. When he was loosed from the sledge on which he was drawn to the gibbet, he sprung up with great alacrity, mounted the steps

> into the cart from which he was to be hung off, and viewed the spectators with as much serenity and as much firmness of mind as if at the head of his company he had been about to give the word of command. Then beckoning to the Sheriff to approach, he told him that he came there to pay his last duty to his king and his country, which he did the more chearfully as he had all along acted in the affair which the Government called the Rebellion according to his conscience; that he died a stedfast tho' unworthy member of the Church of England, heartily repented of his sins, and hoped for forgiveness thro' Christ's merits, but did not reckon that for which he died among the number of his sins, and therefore never did, never would repent of it. In fine, he forgave his enemies and offered up his departing soul to God in the words of our blessed Lord, 'Father into thy hands,' etc.....

He finished his letter with the following thought:

> I may, however, add that he has done the Government more hurt by his death than 40 such lives could have done, and certainly his Majesty was not well advised to take away a life against the inclinations, the wishes, and (if ever the folks of this country did pray), against the prayers too of all ranks and degrees of people, high and low, rich and poor, Whigs and Jacobites; for never were they more united than in their wishes for his safety, nor could there a more acceptable thing been done them than to have spared his life – I am ever, Dear Robin, yours, W.A.
>
> *London, June 12th, 1753.*[161]

Dr Archie lies buried beneath the altar of the Queen's Chapel of the Savoy just off the Strand in London. Part of the Duchy of Lancaster, the chapel belongs to Her Majesty Queen Elizabeth. The plaque in his commemoration lies in the floor on the right hand side of the altar. Now in plain bronze, it replaces a sculpted tablet that was lost in a fire in 1846, which in turn was followed by a stained glass window, blown out by a bomb in the Second World War. The 1745 Association, Mrs Sonia Cameron Jacks, Mrs Victoria Thorpe (members of the Association) and the Duchy of Lancaster were influential in providing this plaque, on which the following is inscribed:

In memory of Doctor Archibald Cameron, brother of Donald Cameron of Lochiel, who having been attainted after the battle of Culloden in 1746 escaped to France but returning to Scotland was apprehended and executed in 1753. He was buried beneath the altar of this Chapel

==============

In Scotland he is remembered in a song written in Gaelic by John Cameron of Dochanassie in 1753. Consisting of seven verses the first runs:

An raoir bruadir mi'n chadal
'S b'fhearr gum faicinn e 'm dhusgadh,
Gun robh thus', a Ghilleasbuig,
Air tighinn a sheasamh do dhuthcha.
Ach 'nuair 'dhuisg mi 's a' mhaduinn
A faoin bhruadar a chadil
Cha d'fhuaras tu agam,
B'fhada, b'fhada bho t'uir thu.

Last night I lay dreaming
What I'd sooner see waking,
*That thou, O Gilleasbuig,**
Hadst come to succour thy country;
But when I awakened
Out of my vain vision,
I could not find thee near me,
Thou wast far from thy country.

**Archibald*

So died the man who has been largely and wrongly forgotten, both for the goodness of his character and his loyalty to the Jacobite cause. Doctor Archie, true to his calling, showed compassion to both friend and foe; his failing, if that it can be called, was his lack of perception of the weakness of others who betrayed him for love of gold.

Archie Cameron, the last man to die for the cause of his exiled Stuart monarch, to him the true British king, deserves to be remembered, not only for the self-sacrifice which led him irrevocably to the scaffold at Tyburn on that day in early June 1753, but also for his unswerving loyalty in the face of such overwhelming odds.

Two letters from famous people give a flavour of the feelings engendered at this execution so long after the Rising had ended: Horace Walpole to Sir Horace Mann, Strawberry Hill, June 12th, 1753:

> Dr Cameron is executed, and died with the greatest firmness. His parting with his wife the night before was heroic and tender: he let her stay till the last moment, when being aware that the gates of the Tower would be locked, he told her so; she fell at his feet in agonies: he said, *'Madam, this was not what you promised me,'* and embracedher, forced her to retire, then with the same coolness, looked at the window till her coach was out of sight, after which he turned about and wept. His only concern seemed to be at the ignominy of Tyburn: he was not disturbed at the dresser for his body, or at the fire to burn his bowels. The crowd was so great, that a friend who attended him could not get away, but was forced to stay and watch the execution: but what will you say to the minister or priest who accompanied him? The wretch, after taking leave, went into a landau, where not content with seeing the doctor hanged, he let down the top of the landau for the

better convenience of seeing him embowelled!* I cannot tell you positively that what I hinted of this Cameron being commissioned from Prussia was true, but so it is believed'.[162]

From Tobias Smollett:

> The populace, though not very subject to tender emotions, were moved to compassion, and even to tears, by his behaviour at the place of execution; and many sincere well wishers to the present establishment thought that the sacrifice of this victim, at such a juncture, could not redound either to its honour or security.

So what was the real reason for which Doctor Archie came to Scotland in the autumn of 1752? According to an unnamed biographer of his day, about three years previously a collection had been made:

> among those who were friends to the Pretender's cause, for the support of his unhappy adherents abroad. Doctor Cameron then came over to England to receive a part of this contribution. Another collection had been set on foot for the same purpose, and the Doctor made instances to his friends here in England for a part in the same, representing by his letters that his pay in the army was not sufficient for him and his numerous family. But after many solicitations, not receiving any satisfactory answer, came over himself; and this was the business that brought him to Scotland, when he was discovered and brought to London.[163]

*Editor's note. There is no indication elsewhere that the Reverend James Falconar's behaviour was anything other than exemplary. In fact, he wrote a very long and detailed account of the Doctor's end for Bishop Forbes, and the note about him in *The Lyon in Mourning* (Vol. III pp. 139-140) runs thus: The Revd Mr James Falconar, a Scots, nonjurant, Episcopal clergyman, residing in London, and who attended the Dr the last four days of his life. Mr Falconar writes this to me (London August 10 1753), *inter alia:* 'May you, nor I, nor none we wish *(continued)*

Was this the reason? Or was it, as some of Archie Cameron's connections in Europe, amongst them Young Edgar when writing to his father asserted, that he went to fetch the gold?

But if this was the case, why did he go to the Trossachs, far from Lochaber when, as he must have known, Cluny had moved the hoard which he himself had buried and re-buried near Loch Arkaig some seven years before.

Or was it, in fact, as Young Glengarry declared, to sound out the possibility of raising the clans for renewed rebellion specifically on the order of Prince Charles?

Archie himself had said *'that he did not come over with a political design, but only to transact some affairs relating to Lochiel's estate'.*[164] And there perhaps we should leave speculation, for that is what Archie himself implies in those last five covertly written pages.

well or who wish us well, ever have such another scene to act as I had on that melancholy yet glorious occasion. I was obliged (indeed, by his own desire) to go to the very gallows with my ever dear friend, and I had almost rather been hanged with him than be witness to his death. But he kept up my spirits, or otherwise I should never have been able to go through with my office.'

Chapter 45
AFTERMATH

In a letter to her husband, written from Edinburgh in 1747 just before Jean left to join him in France, she mentions six children, four boys and two girls. Bel, or Isobel, is believed to have died before James was born in 1751. However, the compiler of *The family of Dr. Archibald Cameron and of his wife Jean,* housed in the Lochaber Archives, states that *'there is evidence that there were seven children alive at the time of their father's execution'.* Who then was the seventh? Was it a boy named Charles? This seems evident from Charles's known entry into the College of Douai and the *'two sons in the French army'* to whom Jean later referred. If this be the case it must be taken that the child she was carrying when she joined Archie in the Tower, which must have been born about a month after his execution, was either stillborn or did not long survive, something hardly surprising in view of what she had endured.

All that is known for certain is that shortly before, or just after the birth, Jean returned to live in France. In January 1754 she wrote from Paris to James Edgar, King James's secretary. Making much use of capital letters she told him that: *'his Majestie's Good and humain Subjects in England gave me as much as I have bore my no Small charges at London and here, and may be good management serve till my pension is payable two years hence'.* The pension she referred to was from the Court of France, *'twelve hundred livres to me and four hundred to each of my two sons in the French Service.'* Two years later she again mentions the pension of *'twelve hundred livres which by Reductions at payment very little exceeds a thousand'.*[165]

Badly off as she was, her letters prove help from friends and relations...*'all such as took any interest in me or my family, particularly Mr. MacPherson of Clunie my Cousin who has acted not only a friendly but a fatherly part and readily came under some engagements with me which were necessary otherwise I should have been at a loss what hand to apply to'.*[166]

Despite Cluny's help Jean was forced to leave her home. Writing to James Edgar in 1756, she said:

> I am obliged to give up my house notwithstanding that Mr Murray, Lord Elibank's brother, pays the rent of it, I am not able to keep it nor live in any way but a Convent in some of the Provinces separate from my poor children who are all the comfort I have left me.[167]

One last letter to James Edgar, written from Calais on 6th September 1759, tantalizingly gives no news either of her family or of herself. Whether she did go into a convent will never be known.

In October 1767 both the *Gentleman's Magazine* and the *Scots Magazine* contained the following death-notice:

> At Ghent Miss Jenny Cameron famous for her attachment to the young Pretender.

Miss Jennie Cameron of Glendessary, supposed mistress of Prince Charles, was of course the same lady who had shared a coach to Stirling with the infamous Samuel Cameron, betrayer of Doctor Archie. Known to have died at her home, Mount Cameron, in 1772, she cannot conceivably have ended her life in Flanders. Therefore it must have been Jean Cameron whose death was reported five years later in Ghent.

The archives of Ogilvie's Regiment show that a Donald and a Charles Cameron were promoted Lieutenants in 1756. Both young men fought in the campaigns of 1760 and 1761 in Germany and are described as *'Bon sujet, fort rangé'*.

John married Elizabeth Hamilton at St Omer on 13th July 1754, apparently to his mother's displeasure because his bride had become a Catholic. Ogilvie's Regiment was disbanded in March 1763, but a John Cameron, colonel in the French Service, died in Edinburgh in 1783.

Archie Cameron's second son Donald (he who petitioned Queen Victoria to place a Plaque to his father in the Savoy Chapel) returned to England to become a partner in the banking house of Harley, Cameron and Son, George Street, Mansion House, London, before being made Sheriff of Essex in 1791. Archie's only surviving daughter Margaret (little Peggy) came back to Scotland to marry Captain Donald Cameron of Strone. Of the other four children nothing is known.[168]

Of Lochiel's family his eldest son John remained in the French army until 1759. Returning home to Scotland he died in Edinburgh of a lingering illness in October 1762.

The younger brother who followed him managed to get leases of parts of the forfeited estates on easy terms from the crown. A soldier too for most of his life, he died in 1776.

Lochiel's brother, John of Fassifern, the burgess of Glasgow, who had implored him not to join the Prince, was charged with having abstracted documents connected with the forfeited estates of Lochiel. Although spared the destruction of his house and land, he was banished from Scotland for ten years – just for being a Cameron.

Lochgarry, Alasdair Ruadh of Glengarry's thoroughly loyal cousin who, in his middle fifties had fled with Prince Charles to France, stayed there for the rest of his life. His wife, Isobel, escaped from her home just as Cumberland and his soldiers broke through the gates to burn the old castle to the ground. Disguised as a workman, with their three sons, she managed to join her husband in France. The two eldest boys got commissions in Ogilvie's Regiment (the *Garde Ecossaise*) and the youngest in the Swiss Guard.

Cluny MacPherson, always loyal to the core, is believed to have taken all that remained of the gold buried at Loch Arkaig to France in 1765. Penniless himself, he died soon afterwards, longing always for Strathspey, heartbroken like his cousin Lochiel.

Thus Doctor Archie, the gentle mannered, peaceful practitioner, who begged his brother not to rise in arms, was proved correct in his prediction that a rising in Scotland could only bring devastation to all those whom it involved. His death did not go unavenged, however. Samuel Cameron, the cousin who finally betrayed him, was a lieutenant in Lord Lewis Drummond's regiment in France, and a note in *The Lyon in Mourning* states that '*Upon Mrs Cameron's going over to France, after her husband's death, the said Samuel Cameron was tried by court-martial and thrown into a dungeon'.* Drummed out of the French Army and afraid to return to the Continent, he ultimately disappeared.

As for 'Pickle', all that is known about his later life is that he lingered on, spurned by his relations, a lonely and impoverished man. Winter in the Highlands comes early. Snow was blowing down from the mountains when, two days before Christmas, 1761, he died beside the ruins of his ancestral castle, in his little 'hutt'.

There were many disgruntled men in Scotland whose belief in the cause of the Stuarts had been shattered by the aftermath of the last two Risings. Among them were those left destitute without any hope of recompense for all that they and their families had endured. While it is hard to exonerate Alasdair Ruadh, in view of the evidence against him perhaps it is only fair to believe that some of it may have been attached to his name simply because he was the known suspect, while others, with a less high profile, were in fact undetected spies. Jean Cameron was certain that he had betrayed her husband, and publicly denounced him after Archie's death.

It is also worth remembering the determination of the Hanoverian Government to eliminate the leaders of the Cameron clan and their adherents, recognizing their primary part in the rising of 1745, and of the equal determination of the Duke of Argyll not to give any quarter to Doctor Archibald Cameron, despite the strenuous efforts of the number of people who begged for his life.[169] Like James of the Glen in Appin, hanged unjustly less than a year before him, Doctor Archie was undoubtedly made a scapegoat by a Government keen to subdue any chance of another rising by enforcing its iron hand.

The cartoonist Hogarth, famous for his depictions of the raffish side of Georgian society, one day called upon his friend Samuel Richardson, author of the novel *Clarissa.* Bursting out with the latest item of public scandal, he informed him that:

> Certainly there must have been some very unfavourable circumstances lately discovered in Doctor Cameron's case, which had induced the King to approve of his execution for rebellion, so long after it was committed, as this had the appearance of putting the man to death in cold blood, and was very unlike his usual clemency.

As he was speaking, Hogarth noticed an extraordinary looking man standing in the window, '*shaking his head, and rolling himself about in a strange and ridiculous manner'.* Thinking him to be some poor, demented relation for whom Richardson was caring, he was much surprised when the figure strode away from the window to deliver an invective against George II '*as one who, upon all occasions, was unrelenting and barbarous ... in short, the peculiar figure displayed such a power of eloquence, that Hogarth looked at him with astonishment, and actually imagined that this idiot had been at the moment inspired'.* Doctor Johnson, for it was he, and Hogarth were not introduced to each other on this occasion. Alexander MacKenzie records that Boswell, Johnson's biographer, added this footnote:

> Impartial posterity may perhaps be as little inclined as Doctor Johnson was to justify the uncommon rigour exercised in the case of Doctor Archibald Cameron. He was an amiable and truly honest man, and his offence was owing to a generous, though mistaken principle of duty. Being obliged, after 1746, to give up his profession as a physician and to go into foreign parts, he was honoured with the rank of Colonel both in the French and Spanish service.[170]

From this it is evident that the money Doctor Cameron was accused of stealing was used, almost entirely, for the support of his dead brother's family. Miss Henrietta Tayler, in a footnote to a letter which is printed in her 'Jacobite Epilogue' says:

> One of the mysterious allusions to the Locharkaig treasure, the full accounts of which exist only among the papers at Windsor, and have not yet been published in extensor. They certainly show that both Cluny and Archibald Cameron were guiltless of peculation.....[171]

How anyone can have doubted Archie's veracity in the first place is the question that at once springs to mind. Archie Cameron stands out as a victim of manipulation from both contemporary and later accounts. His own family was sacrificed. As a doctor it must have been particularly dreadful for him to learn that two of his children had died, either from illness or malnutrition, while he, not far away but tied by his service to Prince Charles, was unable to help them.

The rights and wrongs of the Rising of 1745 have long been, and will continue to be, a source of argument in future years. Some claim that it would never have happened had Lochiel listened to his brothers' arguments and refused to rise. And the brother who, with much initial reluctance, did rise, was the last to die for the Jacobite cause. Archie Cameron stands out as a man whose integrity, loyalty and steadfastness were at the very core of his being.

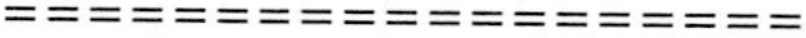

The Plaque in the Queen's Chapel of the Savoy remembering Doctor Archie

Appendix I

The sum of £40 appears in the estimated cost of employing a surgeon, and although Doctor Archibald Cameron was appointed after the York Building Company went bankrupt and the mines were being worked by Francis Grant, merchant in Edinburgh, the brother of Sir Archibald Grant of Moneymusk, the entry in Grant's account book for 28th July 1738 reads 'Bill to John Richardson payed Whitsunday value of Doct. Cameron £46.0.0.' (Ref.GD 345/894/27/3).

MS 3735 F.328 (or 359) is a wadset for two properties in Morvern granted by John Cameron of Glendessary to himself dated 22nd October 1740, and written and witnessed by Archie, who was a counter-signatory for Cameron of Glendessary transactions.

=====================

Appendix II

Dr Archibald Cameron's Memorial Concerning the Locharkaig Treasure
(Stuart Papers. Vol.300, No 80 Circa 1750)

An accompt of 35,000 Louis D'ors sent from France and landed on the West Highlands of Scotland the beginning of May 1746 by order of Sr. Thomas Sheridan and Mr Murray Secretary to H.Royal Highness and taken in charge by Murray who continued in the Countrey as it was resolved to go again to arms.

Stolen in time of landing when the French vessels that carry'd it was ingaged with English Men of war by a fellow who went abroad in one of those ships whose name was conceal'd by the Priest who had it from him in confession 800

Given by Mr Murray to different Corps of the Army fo arrear due some months before, also towards charges to bring up their men to a rendezvous against a day appointed according to concert.

4,200

Caryd south by Mr Murray and lodged in Mr Mc Douels hand att Edr. 3,000

H.R. Highness in Sepr. 1746 brought abroad

3,000

11,000

Remains after

Subtracting the 11,000 out of the 35,000 which 24,000 Louis was given in charge by H.R.H. to Clunie and Angus Cameron, Brother to Glenevis, was desired to be ane assistant trusted under Clunie being his neighbour. Clunie was to remove the money to his own Countrey after parting with H.H. the Acct. of which will best appear by the sFubjoined Copy of one sent by Cluny the original having been shown to His Majesty.

24,000

Copy of Clunies Acct. of the 24,000 Louis

To different setts of people as per particular directions in Writing. 750

In Angus Camerons hand 3,000

To John Cameron of Fasfern to pay of the run by Cess and stipens of Locheils Estate. 350

Given to some of my own friends first on account of my own safety and next on account that the houses of severalls of them were burned and their cattle carried away. I was necessitate to layout the following sume upon them to keep them in good humour, for all the Countreys in Scotland that were concerned in this affair, were turned my Enemys, on account of their being strongly impresse, that all his money had been left in my Custody with particular orders from himself to divide and distribute it amongst such as were concerned in his cause, but in place of answers H.Highnesses directions and as everything had turned out wrong. I was (as they apprehended) to keep and retain all for my private use, and a great many of the people have even to this day the same uncharitable and unjust notion running in their heads by being on this unlucky situation I durst not venture to shelter or skulk among such as were formerly my friends yea my relations and well wishers, and it may be judged had I been lost my whole charge and trust had gone alongst with me att the same time I have taken bills for the throng of the money, not knowing that the same may be hereafter demanded. 500

To Fasfern for his expenses and in order to Enable him to Lable the claims upon Lochiels estate 100

To Major Kennedy*, 6,000

To McPherson of Breachachy who went with the money To Kennedy 600

Exausted in support of myself, necessary Servants, Secretarys, and trustees, and for the subsistence of my Wife, Family and Children for the space of four years 1,200

To intaick in the money and part of it that was Lost and never recovered 481

12,981

Amongst other sources, Lord Amulree states that Cameron has been accused, almost certainly unjustly, of having removed about 6,000 Louis for his own use.... He took what he thought he was entitled to help '*the ruined family of Lochiel*' and also some 300 for his own expenses.

*Kennedy, apparently a racing man, was accused of gambling this away at Newmarket.

The two accounts are dissimilar to the point where the only common figure is that of 6,000. If Cameron gave that sum to Major Kennedy, it was probably for the use of his nephew Lochiel. If, as he says, he took 1,200 for his own family it was hardly an exorbitant sum over the space of four years.

Some of Doctor Archie's memorial is missing but to Clunie's account is added:

Clunie proposed to Archie as he had taken upon him the remaining 5,000 for himself that *Archie should give him a letter as if he had taken the 6,000* designed for Lochiel att his own hand out of the place Archie knew the money lay formerly in, which Archie was so well natured as to do, as Clunie was only to show it to the King if needful, and Archie was going directly to H.Majesty with ane account of it all, *the real fact is* that Archie did not know where Clunie removed the money to after the Prince came abroad as appears by Clunie's acct. sent the King, further severals who were present knows that Archie saw none of it except the 300 Louis Clunie sent for and that Archie parted with Clunie and came south, Clunie brought Fasfern north to receive the 5,700 Louis, this is what will turn out true.....Clunie MacPherson, himself, in a written statement stated as follows.

By Cash given to Dr Cameron and Fassiefern secured with Fassiefern for use of young Lochiel 6,000

In May 1753, Fassiefern himself, then a prisoner in Edinburgh Castle, was examined. He admitted that in 1749 he received 4,000 from Evan Cameron of Drumsallie, now dead, for Lochiel's family. He asked no questions but deposited it with Mr Macfarlane, W.S., who lent it out to Wedderburn of Gosford, in Fassiefern's name. Fassiefern acted as a near relation for his exiled nephew, Lochiel's son.

Notes

1 MacKenzie, Alexander. *History of the Camerons with genealogies of the principal families of that name.* p.208.
2 Ibid. p.206.
3 Burton, John Hill. *Simon Lord Lovat* p.173
4 MacKenzie, Alexander. p.205.
5 Ibid. p.21.
6 Campbell, Robert *The Life of John Duke of Argyll and Greenwich* pp.188-190 and *The Life of John Duke of Argyle p.137*
7 Ibid.
8 Ibid.
9 Henderson, Alexander *Memoirs of Dr Archibald Cameron, brother to the famous Donald Cameron of Lochiel.* p.10.
10 Ibid.
11 Ibid.
12 Ibid. pp.11-12
13 Ibid. pp.12-13
14 Paper on *Doctor Archibald Cameron by Lord Amulree,* published by The Welcome Trust Centre for the History of Medicine at UCL Journal homepage.
15 Ibid. p.231.
16 Ibid.
17 John Stewart of Ardvorlich, *The Camerons.* p.135.
18 Henderson. Alexander pp. 5-6.
19 Ibid. pp. 7-9.
20 Ibid. p.11
21 MacKenzie, Alexander, pp.214-15.
22 Ibid. pp.215-16
23 Ibid.
24 Henderson, Alexander. p.18.
25 Ibid. p.16.
26 Haldane, A.R.B. *The Drove Roads of Scotland.* p. 135.
27 John Stewart of Ardvorlich, *The Camerons* p.135.
28 Amulree, Lord. p.232.
29 Ibid. p.232.
30 National Archives of Scotland
31 *New Statistical Account of Scotland. Argyll.* p.143.
32 *Records of Argyll and the Isles* . I p.304.
33 Monsignor Thomas Wynne *The Forgotten Cameron of the '45* pp.26-7.
34 Gibson, John S. *The Gentle Lochiel.* p.17.

35 Lang, Andrew. *The Companions of Pickle:* p.221.
36 Halloran. B.M. *The Scots College Paris 1603 – 1792.* p.159.
37 Ibid.
38 Maclean, Sir Fitzroy, *Bonnie Prince Charlie* p.31.
39 Gibson, John. S. *The Gentle Lochiel.* P.31.
40 John Murray of Broughton. *Publications of the Scottish History Society Vol. XXVII*
41 Ibid.
42 Ibid
43 Ibid.
44 Gibson. John. S. *The Gentle Lochiel* p.33.
45 Daiches, David. *Charles Edward Stuart* p.108.
46 *An Historical Account of the Life, actions and conduct of Dr Archibald Cameron, brother to Donald Cameron of Lochiel, chief of that clan Containing the reasons which induced the doctor to list himself among the rebels.*
47 Henderson, Alexander. p.23.
48 Amulree, Lord. p.233.
49 John Murray of Broughton .
50 Ibid.
51 Daiches, David
52 Murray p.134.
53 Gibson. John. S. *The Gentle Lochiel.* p.47.
54 Henderson, Alexander. pp.25-6
55 Family History of the Murray Threiplands of Fingask
56 Henderson, Alexander.
57 *'A Plain, General and Authentic Account of the Conduct of the Rebels, during their stay in Derby'*, reprinted in *Historical Papers Relating to the Jacobite Period* (New Spalding Club) p.288.
58 Ibid. p.230
59 Chambers R. *History of the Rebellion in Scotland 1745-46.* Vol. II. pp.12-13.
60 Amulree, Lord. p.234
61 Constable. *History of the Rebellion in Scotland 1745-1746.* pp.7-16.
62 From the Cluny Charter Chest, as published in Vol. XXI of the *Transactions of the Gaelic Society of Inverness.* The letter was written from "Glenevese" (Cameron of Glennevis). Glen Nevis was the base of operations for the siege of Fort William.

63 The Cameron Archives. Letter to Prince Charles Edward Stuart by Donald 'The Gentle Lochiel' XIX Chief of Clan Cameron, and MacDonald of Keppoch, March 20th , 1746.

64 Fergusson, Sir James. *Argyll in the Forty-Five*. pp.99-100.

65 Ibid. p.142.

66 Ibid. p.121.

67 Ibid. p.144.

68 Chambers Robert, p.83.

69 An Historical Account of the Life of Dr Archibald Cameron

70 Amulree, Lord. p.14.

71 John Murray of Broughton pp.10-181

72 Ibid.

73 MacLean, Sir Fitzroy p.231

74 Murray of Broughton

75 Cumberland Papers. *Memoir from Colonel Napier.*

76 Gibson, John S. *The Gentle Lochiel* p.66

77 Amulree, Lord. p.234.

78 Gibson, John. S. *The Gentle Lochiel* p.66.

79 Ibid. p.71

80 Fergusson, Sir James. *Argyll in the Forty-Five*. p.211.

81 *Campbell of Mamore, MSS*. 396. pp.91,93, 94.

82 Mackenzie, Alexander. p.178.

83 Fergusson, Sir James. p.208.

84 H.M. Register Office Edinburgh. Anonymous letter, written in pencil, headed *Dr Archibald Cameron.*

85 Chambers. R. Vol.II. p.219.

86 Ibid.

87 Ibid.

88 Ibid. p.221.

89 Ibid. p.223.

90 Ibid. p.224.

91 Ibid. pp.224-5

92 Maclean, Sir Fitzroy. p.279

93 Gibson, John S. *Ships of the '45* p.134

94 Chambers, R. p.227

95 Gibson, John S. *Ships of the '45* p.134

96 Forbes, Bishop Robert, *The Lyon in Mourning* Vol. I p.216

97 Ibid.

98 *The Family of Doctor Archibald Cameron and his wife Jean p.18*

99 Wynne, Monsignor Thomas. *The Forgotten Cameron of the'45* pp. 84-5.
100 Ibid, p.87.
101 Daiches, David. p.262.
102 Maclean, Sir Fitzroy, p.301.
103 Daiches, David. p. 265.
104 Amulree, Lord. p.235.
105 Mackenzie, Alexander. pp 241-2.
106 Gibson, John S. *The Gentle Lochiel.* p.84.
107 Amulree, Lord, p.235.
108 Mackenzie, Alexander. p.249.
109 Ibid. pp. 247-49
110 Ibid. pp .248-9.
111 Maclean. Sir Fitzroy. p. 303.
112 Lochaber Archive Centre. Typescript of *The family of Doctor Archibald Cameron and of his wife Jean etc.* pp.3-4.
113 Ibid.
114 Ibid.
115 *The Family of Doctor Archibald Cameron and of his wife Jean etc.* Register House Edinburgh. Document CL/B/43/9/1.
116 Amulree, Lord. p.236.
117 Gibson, John S. *The Gentle Lochiel.* p.87
118 Mackenzie, Alexander. pp.251-2.
119 Ibid. pp. 252-3.
120 Ibid. p. 253.
121 Ibid. pp. 264-5.
122 Ibid.
123 Lang, Andrew. *Pickle the Spy.* p.93.
124 Ibid. p.99.
125 Ibid. pp.94-95.
126 Ibid. pp.139-40
127 Amulree, Lord. p.236.
128 Lang Andrew. *The Companions of Pickle etc.* pp.153-4.
129 Ibid. p.95.
130 Mackenzie, Alexander. pp.265-6.
131 Lang, Andrew. *Pickle the Spy* .p.96
132 Ibid. pp.96-7.
133 Amulree,Lord. p.237.
134 Ibid.
135 Lang, Andrew. *The Companions of Pickle.* pp.133-4.

136 Ibid.
137 Ibid . p.138.
138 Mackenzie, Alexander. pp.266-7.
139 Ibid.
140 Lang, Andrew. *Pickle the Spy*. pp.106-108.
141 Henderson, Alexander. p.35.
142 Lang, Andrew. *Pickle the Spy*. p.148.
143 Amulree, Lord, p.237.
144 MacKenzie, Alexander. p.292.
145 Lang, Andrew. *The Companions of Pickle.* p.141.
146 Amulree, Lord. p.238.
147 Ibid.
148 An Historical Account of the Life of Dr Archibald Cameron
149 Lang, Andrew.
150 *The letters of Horace Walpole, Earl of Orford*. Vol.2. pp 164 & 166.
151 Lang, Andrew. *Pickle the Spy*. pp 108-110.
152 Ibid. p.124.
153 Amulree, Lord. pp 238-9
154 Ibid. p.126.
155 Henderson A. Memoirs etc. pp.40-41
156 Ibid.
157 Bishop Forbes *The Lyon in Mourning* Vol. III pp.132-37
158 Doctor Cameron's letters were inherited by Thomas Cameron, vicar of Heckington in Lincolnshire, from his great grandfather Thomas Cameron, the only son of the Reverend John Cameron, evicted non-juring incumbent of Kincardine, who was resident in Edinburgh when Archibald Cameron was a student.
159 Bishop Forbes *The Lyon in Mourning* Vol. III pp.139-40 (footnote)
160 Amulree, lord
161 Bishop Forbes Vol. III pp.130-31
162 Walpole, Horace, Vol 2. p.174
163 Anonymous contemporary biographer.
164 *The family of Doctor Archibald Cameron and his wife Jean,* p.18
165 Ibid.
166 Ibid.
167 Ibid.
168 Mackenzie, Alexander, pp.277-8.
169 Ibid. pp.276-7.
170 Tayler, Henrietta, *Jacobite Epilogue* – footnote to a letter.
171 Bishop Forbes, Vol.III p.134 (footnote)

INDEX

Abernethie, Reverend William, 197
Achnacarry, 1,6,8,10,13,15, 21-2,56,63,94-5,101,124
Act of Union, 36
Airlie, Earl of, 153
Albemarle, Lord, 129,142
Anderson, Robert, 73
Argyll, Duke of, 12,88,92,104,171,207
Atholl Brigade, 91
Austrian Succession, War of, 36,136,142

Bannockburn , battle of, l 82
Barbara, Infanta of Portugal, 139
Bastille Sainte Antoine, 143
Bautista de Toledo, Juan, 139
Beaulieu-Trehouard, Capitaine, 124
Bedford, Colonel, 91
Belleisle, Marshal de, 137
Ben Alder, 112-3,122-3
Berwick, Duke of, 11
Billingsley, Mr Case, 38
Bland, Major-General, 103
Blair, John, 20
Boerhaave, Professor, 21
Breadalbane, John Earl of, 11
Brett, Colonel, 167
Burt, Captain, 31,34

Cameron, Alan, 116
Cameron, Allan, 5,28,66
Cameron, Father Alexander, 15,17 21,44-5,66,111,113,128-30
Cameron, Anne,*(wife of Donald, 'the Gentle Lochiel')* 11,26,60,63,141
Cameron, Doctor Archibald(Archie) Childhood 15, education 17, in Paris 20, Leyden 21, qualifies as doctor 21, 'civilization' of clan 23-5, assistance to General Wade 31, his strength 33, loved by the people 34, medical knowledge 34-6, involvement with York Building Company 38,41, cousin to Colin Campbell of Glenure 41-2,171, children 44,

Cameron, Doctor Archie (continued) opposition to Rising 56, meeting with Prince 57, change of mind 61-2, preparations for war 62, Glenfinnan 64, attack on Ruthven Barracks 68, his selfless care of all wounded 74, disagreement with brother 80, influence in background 81, wounded 93, attending battle wounded 91-3, in search of the Prince 96, involvement with Loch Arkaig Gold 98-101, 158,163, at Strontian and home burnt 104,110, fear for children 111, Loch Sheil 105-6, family worries 113, at Ben Alder searching for Prince 115, at Cluny's Cage 120, shocked at desolation 121, journey to Loch nan Uamh 123-4, departure 125, exile 126-7, physician to regiment 133, visit with Prince to Spain 136-8, imprisonment in Bastille 143, letters to King James 48-9,145-6, regimental connections 133,153, first covert visit to Scotland 154, Young Glengarry's calumny 155-8, resulting actions 159, serious illness 159-10, Douai 165, second visit 170, escapes capture 171, Appin murder 172, betrayal 173-4,'Mr Chalmers' 175, capture 177, imprisonment 184, farewell to Jean 197, execution 197, burial 198
Sons of Doctor Archie:
Allan, 141
Donald 141,204-5
Duncan 141
John, 20th Chief, 141-2 44,46-7,149,205

Daughters of Doctor Archie:
Bel (Isobel) 141
Peggy, 9,141,205
Cameron, Charles, architect, 160
Cameron, Euan, 9,15,17,20-1,44
Cameron, Isobel, *(wife of John Cameron 18th Chief) 1,21*
Cameron, James,160,185,203
Cameron, Jean, of Dungallon,*(wife of Dr Archie) 16,*22,36, 40-1,104-5, 110,126,134,141-3, 158,160.162,164,171, 185-7,194,203-4,206
Cameron, Jennie, 64,204
Cameron, John, Presbyterian Minister, 61,66,93
Cameron of Clunes,113,116,123
Cameron of Dochanassie, 199
Cameron of Dungallon, Alexander. 41,61,66,105,107,162
Cameron of Dungallon, Archibald,16,162
Cameron of Dungallon, Mrs *(Jean's mother)* 40,104,110
Cameron of Fassifern,15,26,57-8, 127,168,205
Cameron of Glendessary,10,17,204
Cameron of Glennevis, Alexander, 162-3,168,173,210
Cameron of Glennevis, Samuel,6,16,134,155,162, 164-5,173-4,204,206
Cameron of Kinloch, 75
Cameron of Lochiel, Donald, 19th Chief (the Gentle Lochiel)(23), saw change must come 25, letter from King James 27, helped General Wade31-2, (46,52,54-5), first visit to Prince 58-9, the march to Glenfinnan 64, (66), enters Edinburgh70,(77-9), Lady Lochiel's servants murdered 81, injured at Falkirk 83, (86), last visit to Achnacarry 95,(97). Fear for his home's survival103, hides on island 104, leaves same just in time 108, meets with Cluny111-2,
Cameron of Lochiel, Donald (continued) in hiding 116-7, at the 'Cage' 121, departure from Loch nan Uamh124, writes to King James133, begs Prince to write to his father138, final illness and death144,(153,)
Cameron of Lochiel, Sir Ewen, 17th Chief,1- 7,15
Cameron of Lochiel, John, 18th Chief, 1,8-10,12-15,21,128
Cameron of Torcastle, Ludovic, 24-5,66,98,143,159
Campbell, Governor Archibald, 63
Campbell, Major-General John, 88,104,107
Campbell of Auchinbreck, 11,26
Campbell of Auchindoun, 88
Campbell of Barcaldine, Patrick, 41
Campbell of Glenure, Colin, 41, 94, 171
Campbell of Lochnell, Alexander,1
Campbell of Lochnell, Sir Duncan 151
Campbell of Lochnell, Lady Duncan 190
Campbell of Octomore, Governer of Castle Stalker 87
Campbell of Shawfield, 190
Campbell of Stonefield, 87-8,107
Carlisle,78
Carlyle Alexander,74
Carvajal, Jose de, y Lancaster, 139, 187
Charles II, 24
Charteris. 169
Chevalier de St George, 10
Clans: Cameron, 3,7,12,16,23,66, 73,86,103,144,212,216,222
Fraser, 91
Gordon, 162
MacDonald, 6,73,86,103,122
MacDonell of Glengarry,28,67
Clan Chattan (MacIntosh, MacGillivray, MacLachlan, MacLean, MacBean etc,) 92,103

Clans: MacMartin *(sept of Clan Cameron),* 4
MacPherson, 25
Stewarts of Appin, 67,73,86,91,260
Clare, Lord, 165
Cluny' Cage, 119-23
General Cope, 73-4
Corrieyairack Pass, 67,115
Craven, Captain, 176-8
Culloden, battle of, 93,97,118,162, 184,199.
Cumberland, William, Duke of, 85, 88-9,95,121,127,136

Derby,78
Dorlaithers, John Gordon, 48
Douglas, Sir John, 169
Drummond of Balhaldie,MacGregor, 6,39,48,141,144,166
Drummond, Lord John, 46,82
Dufresne Marion, Capitaine, 124
Dundee, Viscount, 2
Dunlop, Mister, 18

Edgar, James, 150, 155, 161, 165, 180, 182, 202-4
Edinburgh Castle, 71,77,97,178
Elcho, Lord, 74, 93, 131, 169
Elector of Bavaria ,11
Elector of Hanover, 10-1, 137, 192-3
Elibank, Alexander, 167
Elibank, Lord, 167,169,204
Elibank Plot, 167,180
Earl Marischal, 27,48,167-8,183
Erskine, James, Lord Grange, 178
Erskine of Tinwald, Charles, 160,171

Falkirk, Battle of, 82
Faulkner, General, 107
Father Leslie,151,162
Feile beag, 47
Ferdinand VI, King of Spain, 136-140
Fergussone, Captain John, 107-8,111, 128
Fontenoy, Battle of, 49, 82, 84
Forbes, Bishop Robert, 126, 132,141, 176-7,195,197,201,21920
Frederick, King of Prussia, 168,182

French Ships:
Bellona, 98, Du Teillay, 57
L'Heureux, 124, Mars, 98
Prince de Conti, 124,127

George I, 12
George II, 88,167,207
Glasgow, 80-1
Glencairn's Rising, 29
Gordon, Principal Alexander,181
Gordon of Glenbucket, 101
Gordon, Lord Lewis, 131
Gordon of Park, Sir William, 165
Grant, Peter, 113
Gregoire, 19

Hanoverians, 64,88,91,97,207
Harrison, Sir James, 169
Hay of Restalrig, John, 96
Hawley, General, 82-3
Hepburn of Keith, 169
Hogarth, 207
Holker, John, 161-2
Howard of the Buffs, Colonel, 103
Howard, Thomas, Duke of Norfolk, 38
Houghton, Brigadier, 107
Huntley, Marquis of, 131
Hutchinson, Francis. 18

Innes, George, 47

Jacobites ix,8,12-3,43,49,51,67,70,73-4 79,82,84,89,104,109,129,133 143,152,158,161-2,168,171, 173-4,198,209
James VIII, 5,27,57,72,159,161
Johnson, Doctor Samuel, 208

Keith, General James, 167
Kennedy, Major Ludovick, 99,106,155,164,211-2
Killiecrankie, battle of, 3
Kilmarnock, Lord, 85

Langlands, George, 40
Loch Arkaig Gold, 95,97-8,101,121, 154,157-8,163,212
Loudoun, Lord, 103

Louis XV, King of France,11,46,50,
130-1,133,136
Lovat, Simon Lord, 24,29,46,53-4,
101,103,108,213

Macaulay, Lord, 3
MacBaine, Alexander, 17
MacDonald, Aeneas, Banker,
48,98,1 52,157
MacDonald of Barrisdale, Coll, 99,101
MacDonald of Clanranald ,54,84,99,
101-2,122,151,170
MacDonald, Alexander, of
Glenaladale,122
MacDonald, John, brother to
Glenaladale, 122-3
MacDonald, Sir John, 57,65
MacDonald of Keppoch, 2,54,87,
216,222
MacDonald of Kingsburgh, 173

MacDonald of Kinlochmoidart, 48
MacDonald of Lochgarry, 101,103,
113-4,123-4,154,168,170,205
MacDonald of Sleat, Sir Alexander, 49

MacDonell of Glengarry,
2,29,47,54,66,153
MacDonell, Alasdair Ruadh, Young
Glengarry, 47-8,50,66,
145,150-1,152-3,156-7,
159,161,167,180
MacDonald, Flora, 111
MacGregor, James Mor, 74, 170
MacGregor, Rob Roy, 13
Mclan, Angus, 154
MacLeod of MacLeod, Norman ,46,52
MacMillan, Donald, 40
MacPherson, Cluny, 86,93,112,117-9,
121,123-4,149,153-6,158,
163-4,168,173,203,206
Mar,John, Earl of, 12
Middleton,General, 2
Mirepoix, Duc de, 186
Monk, General, 2
Morrison *(Prince Charles' valet)*,169
Munro, Doctor Alexander, 19
Munro of Foulis, Robert, 84
Murray, Sir Alexander, 38-9,41

Murray of Broughton,40,46,48-9
51,70,90,94,101,109,162,
171,183,214-6,222
Margaret Murray *(wife of above)*
105-6
Murray, Lord George, 74,83,85,90,92
Murray, Lord John, 175

Napier, Colonel, 97,99,163,216,222
Newcastle, Duke of, 129,171,179,
184

Ogilvie,Lord,131,133,153,159,165,
167
O'Sullivan, Colonel, 66-7,89,91,93,138

Palazzo Muti, 158
Pelham, Henry, 151-2,168,187
Perth, Duke of, 12,41, 46,51-2,79,94,175
Philip II, King of Spain, 139
Philiphaugh, battle of, 2
Preston, General, 77
Prestonpans, battle of, 73-4,78
Prince Charles Edward Stuart,
40,46,48-51,54,56-7,61,
63,66-7,70,73,75-9,81-2,
84-6,93-4,105,108,118,120,
122,124,127,130-2,134,136,
138,140,142-4,147,150,153.
155-6.159,162-4,167,169,172,
183,202,204-5,208,216,222
Prince Henry, Duke of York, 133,
150,193
Prestonpans, battle of, 74
Puysieux, Marquis de, 143

Queen Anne, 10-12
Queen's Chapel of the Savoy, 198,205

Reformation, 10
Religion, 10-11,43-4,47,66,100,188,191
Robertson of Wood Streat, 168
Ross, Andrew, 17
Rossi, Mattia de, 158
Royal Scots Regiment, 46,48
Ruthven Barracks, 67

Saxe, Marshal, 49
Schools, 35
Scots College at Douai, 45,166
Scott, Captain Caroline , 88-9,105
Scott, Captain John, 62-3
Scott, Sir Walter, 7
Seymour, Algernon, 7th Duke of
Somerset, 12
Sheridan, Sir Thomas, 96,98
Sherrifmuir, battle of, 12
Simpson, Robert, 18, 48
Sinclair (St Clair) Doctor, 19
Smith, Bishop, 48
Smith, Commodore, 122
Smollett, Tobias, 161,201
Stewart, Alexander, 68
Stewart, Charles, Earl of Traquair,
46,52-3
Stewart, John Roy, 101,123-4
Stewart, James of the Glen, 171,207
Stewart,. Provost of Edinburgh, 70
Stewart of Ardshiel, 54,67,94,106
Stewart of Glenbuckie, 174-5
Stirling Castle, 82,178
Strontian (and Lead Mines) 37-8,40,42,
104-5,106-7

Tartan, 33,69
Threipland, Christian, 77
Threipland, Sir Stuart, vii,75,99,
105,112,116,120
Tower of London, 109,184
Treaty of Aix-la-Chapelle, 143

Wade, General George, 31
Walpole, Horace,181,200,219, 222
Warren, Colonel, 124-5

York Building Company 38,41

BIBLIOGRAPHY

'A Plain, General and Authentic account of the conduct of the Rebels during their stay in Derby' reprinted in *Historical Papers Relating to the Jacobite Period* (New Spalding Club)

Amulree, Lord. Paper on *Dr Archibald Cameron*, published by The Welcome Trust Centre for the History of Medicine at UCL Journal homepage.

An Historical account of *the Life, actions and conduct of Dr Archibald Cameron, brother to Donald Cameron of Lochiel, chief of that clan. Containing the reasons which induced the doctor to list himself among the rebels etc.*

Browne, James. *The History of Scotland* Vol 6: Its Highland Regiments and Clans. Publ. Francis A. Niccolls & Co, Edinburgh, London, Boston.

Campbell of Mamore MSS.

Campbell, Robert. *The Life of John, Duke of Argyll and Greenwich.*

Chambers, R. *History of the Rebellion in Scotland Vol 2. Printed for Constable & Co. and Hurst, Chance & Co., London 1827*

Daiches, David. *Charles Edward Stuart*, Thames & Hudson, London.

Doctor Cameron's letters which were inherited by Thomas Cameron, Vicar of Heckington in Lincolnshire, from his great grandfather Thomas Cameron, the only son of the Revd John Cameron, evicted non-juring incumbent of Kincardine, who was resident in Edinburgh when Archibald Cameron was studying medicine there.

Fergusson, Sir James. *Argyll in the Forty-Five.* Published Faber & Faber, London.

Forbes, Bishop Robert. *The Lyon in Mourning.* Four Volumes Publ. by Scottish Academic Press, Edinburgh 1975

Gibson, John S. *Ships of the '45* Publ. by Hutchinson & Co Ltd. 1967

Gibson, John S. *The Gentle Lochiel.* NMS Publishing United.

H.M. Register Office Edinburgh. Anonymous letter, written in pencil, headed *Dr Archibald Cameron.*

Haldane, A.R.B. *The Drove Roads of Scotland* Publ. by ?????

Halloran, B.M. *The Scots College Paris 1603 – 1792.* John Donald Publishers Ltd, Edinburgh.

Henderson, Alexander. *Memoirs of Dr Archibald Cameron, brother to the famous Donald Cameron of Lochiel*

Lang, Andrew. *Pickle the Spy & Companions of Pickle.* Kessinger Publishing Reprints.

Lang, Andrew. Cumberland Papers. *Memoir for Colonel Napier. Companions of Pickle.*

Lochaber Archive Centre. Typescript of *The Family of Dr Archibald Cameron and of his wife Jean etc.*

Mackenzie, Alexander. *History of the Camerons with genealogies of the principal families of that name.* Publ. Inverness MDCCCLXXXIV

Maclean, Sir Fitzroy. *Bonnie Prince Charlie.* Publ.George Weidenfield & Nicholson Ltd 1988 In paperback Canongate Books Ltd Edinburgh 1989.

Murray of Broughton, John. Publications of the Scottish History Society Vol. XXVII.

New Statistical Account of Scotland, Argyll. Published William Blackwood & Sons, Edinburgh and London MDCCCXLV

Records of Argyll & the Isles.

Stewart of Ardvorlich, John. *The Camerons. A History of Clan Cameron.* Publ. by The Clan Cameron Association 1974

Tayler, Henrietta, *Jacobite Epilogue (footnote)*

The Cameron Archives. Letters to Prince Charles Edward Stuart by Donald 'The Gentle Lochiel' XIX Chief of Clan Cameron, and MacDonald of Keppoch, March 20th 1746

The Cluny Charter Chest, as published in Vol.XXI of the Transactions of the Gaelic Society of Inverness. The letter was written from 'Glenevese' (Cameron of Glennevis). Glen Nevis was the base of operations for the siege of Fort William.

The Family of Dr Archibald Cameron and of his wife Jean etc. Register House Edinburgh. Document CL/B/43/9/1.

The Letters of Horace Walpole, Earl of Orford, Vol.2.

Wynne, Monsignor Thomas. *The Forgotten Cameron of the '45.*

=================

NAIRN
Culloden
INVERNESS
Loch Ness
Ft Augustus
Loch Garry
Invergarry
Corrieyairack Pass
Glenkingie
Loch Arkaig
Achnacarry
Loch Eil
Ft William
Ardgour
Ben Alder
Loch Ericht
Strontian
Loch Linnhe
Ballachulish
L. Rannoch
Loch Etive
Loch Tay
Loch Awe
Brenacoille
L. Katrine
Inversnaid
L. Lomond
Loch Fyne
STIRLING

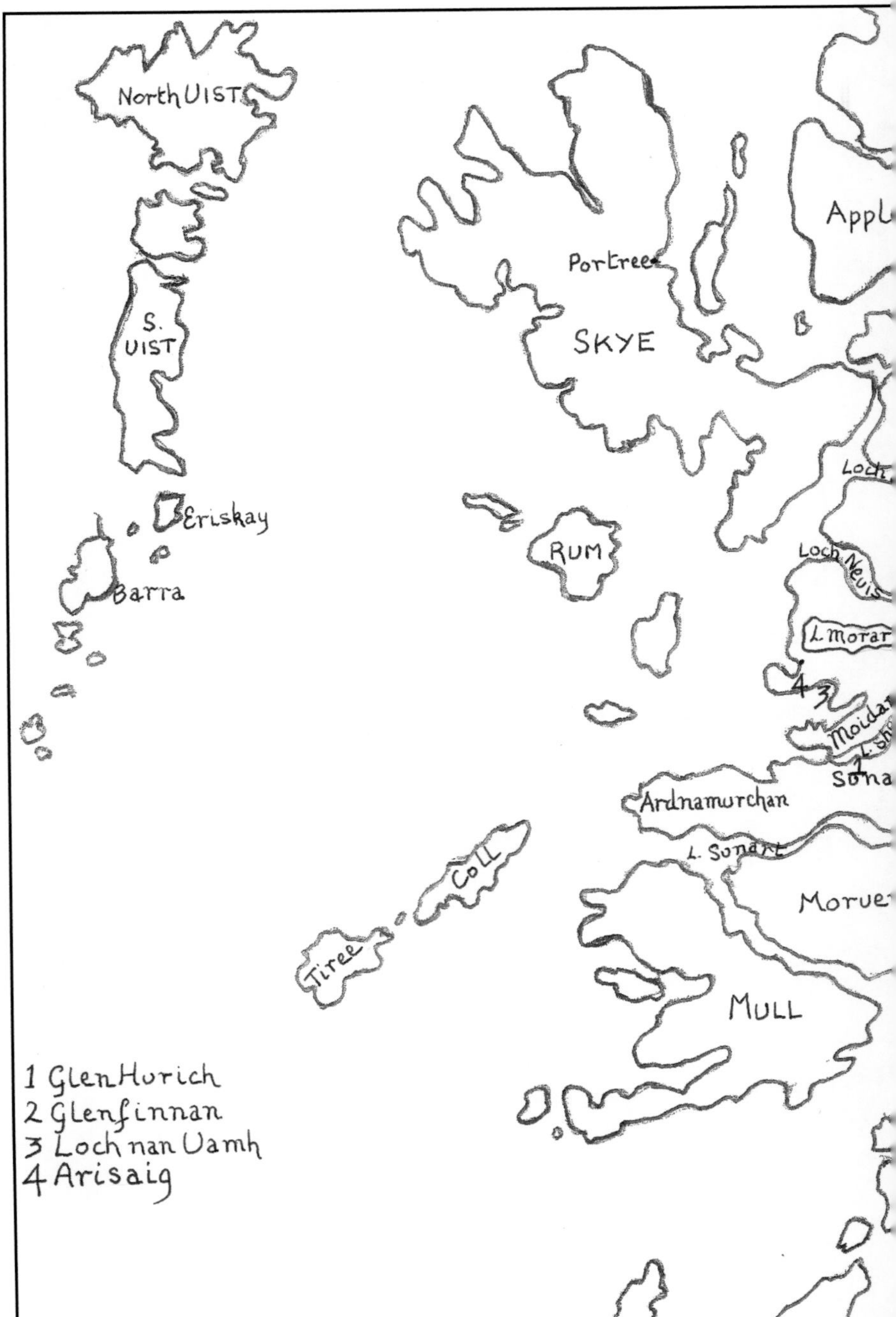
North UIST
S. UIST
Eriskay
Barra
Portree
SKYE
RUM
Loch Nevis
L. Morar
Ardnamurchan
L. Sonart
Coll
Tiree
MULL
1 Glen Horich
2 Glenfinnan
3 Loch nan Uamh
4 Arisaig
SCJ '14